You're Reading in the Wrong Direction!!

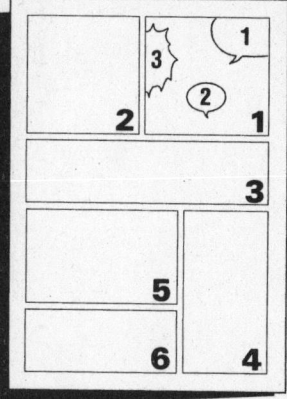

Whoops! Guess what? You're starting at the wrong end of the comic!

…It's true! In keeping with the original Japanese format, **Assassination Classroom** is meant to be read from right to left, starting in the upper-right corner.

Unlike English, which is read from left to right, Japanese is read from right to left, meaning that action, sound effects and word-balloon order are completely reversed… something which can make readers unfamiliar with Japanese feel pretty backwards themselves. For this reason, manga or Japanese comics published in the U.S. in English have sometimes been published "flopped"—that is, printed in exact reverse order, as though seen from the other side of a mirror.

By flopping pages, U.S. publishers can avoid confusing readers, but the compromise is not without its downside. For one thing, a character in a flopped manga series who once wore in the original Japanese version a T-shirt emblazoned with "M A Y" (as in "the merry month of") now wears one which reads "Y A M"! Additionally, many manga creators in Japan are themselves unhappy with the process, as some feel the mirror-imaging of their art skews their original intentions.

We are proud to bring you Yusei Matsui's **Assassination Classroom** in the original unflopped format.
For now, though, turn to the other side of the book and let the adventure begin…!

—Editor

SHOYO HINATA IS OUT TO PROVE THAT IN VOLLEYBALL YOU DON'T NEED TO BE TALL TO FLY

HAIKYU!!

Story and Art by HARUICHI FURUDATE

Ever since he saw the legendary player known as the "Little Giant" compete at the national volleyball finals, Shoyo Hinata has been aiming to be the best volleyball player ever! He decides to join the team at the high school the Little Giant went to—and then surpass him. Who says you need to be tall to play volleyball when you can jump higher than anyone else?

www.viz.com

HAIKYU!! © 2012 by Haruichi Furudate/SHUEISHA Inc.

THE ACTION-PACKED SUPERHERO COMEDY ABOUT ONE MAN'S AMBITION TO BE A HERO FOR FUN!

ONE-PUNCH MAN

STORY BY
ONE

ART BY
YUSUKE MURATA

Nothing about Saitama passes the eyeball test when it comes to superheroes, from his lifeless expression to his bald head to his unimpressive physique. However, this average-looking guy has a not-so-average problem—he just can't seem to find an opponent strong enough to take on!

Can he finally find an opponent who can go toe-to-toe with him and give his life some meaning? Or is he doomed to a life of superpowered boredom?

ONE-PUNCH MAN © 2012 by ONE, Yusuke Murata/SHUEISHA Inc.

www.viz.com

Food Wars! SHOKUGEKI NO SOMA

Saucy, action-packed food battles!

Story by **Yuto Tsukuda**
Art by **Shun Saeki**
Contributor **Yuki Morisaki**

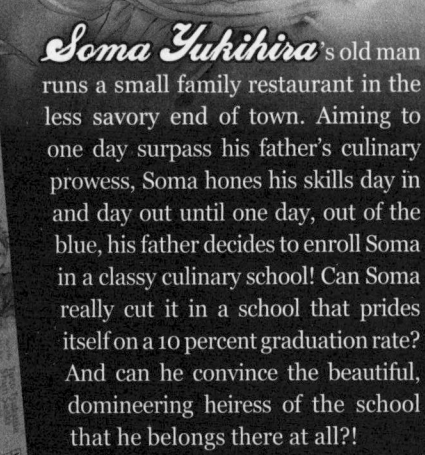

Soma Yukihira's old man runs a small family restaurant in the less savory end of town. Aiming to one day surpass his father's culinary prowess, Soma hones his skills day in and day out until one day, out of the blue, his father decides to enroll Soma in a classy culinary school! Can Soma really cut it in a school that prides itself on a 10 percent graduation rate? And can he convince the beautiful, domineering heiress of the school that he belongs there at all?!

www.viz.com

SHOKUGEKI NO SOMA © 2012 by Yuto Tsukuda, Shun Saeki /SHUEISHA Inc.

YOU'VE READ THE MANGA—NOW WATCH THE ANIME!

ASSASSINATION CLASSROOM | SEASONS 1&2

OWN IT NOW ON BLU-RAY, DVD & DIGITAL HD

FUNIMATION.COM/ASSASSINATIONCLASSROOM

ASSASSINATION
CLASSROOM

Volume 21
SHONEN JUMP ADVANCED Manga Edition

Story and Art by YUSEI MATSUI

Translation/Tetsuichiro Miyaki
English Adaptation/Bryant Turnage
Touch-up Art & Lettering/Stephen Dutro
Cover & Interior Design/Sam Elzway
Editor/Annette Roman

ANSATSU KYOSHITSU © 2012 by Yusei Matsui
All rights reserved.
First published in Japan in 2012 by SHUEISHA Inc., Tokyo.
English translation rights arranged by SHUEISHA Inc.

The stories, characters and incidents mentioned in this
publication are entirely fictional.

No portion of this book may be reproduced or
transmitted in any form or by any means without
written permission from the copyright holders.

Printed in the U.S.A.

Published by VIZ Media, LLC
P.O. Box 77010
San Francisco, CA 94107

10 9 8 7 6 5 4 3 2 1
First printing, April 2018

www.viz.com

www.shonenjump.com

PARENTAL ADVISORY
ASSASSINATION CLASSROOM is rated T+ for Older
Teen and is recommended for ages 16 and up. It
contains realistic violence and suggestive situations.
ratings.viz.com

Well then...goodbye.

– Koro Sensei

Koro Sensei has become the moon.
He steadfastly watches over us through the night and day.
He is our octopus crescent moon.

ASSASSINATION
CLASSROOM

YUSEI MATSUI

TIME TO SAY THANK YOU

As always, the only subject an author can write about in the final volume's author comments is gratitude...

...gratitude for getting the opportunity to work on this series, gratitude for the people who bought it, gratitude to you for reading it all the way through to the very end, gratitude for this once-in-a-lifetime experience, gratitude for the opportunity to meet all of you...

Thank you very much!

–Yusei Matsui

Yusei Matsui was born on the last day of January in Saitama Prefecture, Japan. He has been drawing manga since elementary school. Some of his favorite manga series are *Bobobo-bo Bo-bobo*, *JoJo's Bizarre Adventure* and *Ultimate Muscle*. Matsui learned his trade working as an assistant to manga artist Yoshio Sawai, creator of *Bobobo-bo Bo-bobo*. In 2005, Matsui debuted his original manga *Neuro: Supernatural Detective* in *Weekly Shonen Jump*. In 2007, *Neuro* was adapted into an anime. In 2012, *Assassination Classroom* began serialization in *Weekly Shonen Jump*.

Graphic Novel Editor
Gendai Shoin company: Ryusuke Kuroki

Designer
hive: Tadashi Hisamochi
hive: Seiko Dobashi

Shueisha Rights Department
Susumu Hieda
Kazumasa Sanjoba
Keita Kodama

SCRAP: Takao Kato

nendo: Oki Sato

Kodai Abe

Everyone else involved with
the various products, events
and publications.

All of my friends, family, teachers
and most of all—you!

Once again, thank you very much!

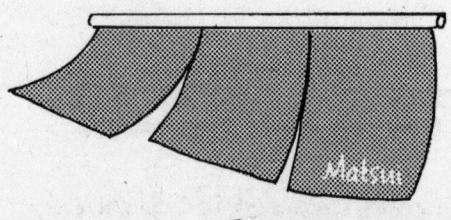

See you again!

Special Thanks

Manga Staff
Kei Nishiyama
Taichi Yokoyama
Takamasa Morii
Masakazu Maehata
Fumio Fukuda

Everybody who helped me with this work.

Editor
Shu Murakoshi

Anime
Director Seiji Kishi,
Producer Noriko Ozaki and
all the other anime staff.

Jun Fukuyama and all the
other anime cast members.

Everyone involved in the Anime.

Movie
Director Eichiro Hasumi,
Producer Juichi Uehara and all
the other movie production crew.

Ryosuke Yamada,
Kazunari Ninomiya and all the
other movie cast members.

Everyone involved in the movie.

TOKYO DEPARTMENT STORE WAR JOURNAL (THE END)

THE BRAT MANAGED TO PROTECT THE WATCH FROM ME.

TCH...

BIG THINGS, SMALL THINGS, LECHEROUS THINGS...

THIS GUY'S DESIRE IS A BOTTOMLESS PIT.

HE WANTS THEM ALL REALLY BADLY AND AT ANY COST.

RST

WH—?!

OH!

WHA—?! THIS...

HOW MUCH... IS IT...?

HMM...

BUT I GUESS...

TWENTY YEARS OLD... WOULD BE ABOUT RIGHT.

...THAT'S WHY HE'S A WILD MERCHANT.

?

THE STRONGER YOUR DESIRE, THE MORE FAITHFUL THE DESIGN OF THE WATCH WILL BE.

EVEN THE ARTWORK IS THE SAME!

THIS...

Custom-Made Wrist Watch

It scans the brain waves of whoever opens the box to determine its final design.

¥6,600,000

...IS DADDY'S...

THAT'S WHY I ASKED YOU TO SAY IT OUT LOUD.

...!

...

...!!

I THINK I KIND OF GET IT NOW...

...

SHFF

GIMME!

ACTUALLY, THAT ARTWORK IS PRETTY NICE...

!

I...
JUST...

IS IT THAT DIFFICULT A FEELING TO UNDERSTAND?

LITTLE LADY...

WHAT DOES IT REALLY MEAN TO DESIRE?

BLUGG

A CUSTOMER... APPROACHING AT CLOSE RANGE...

WOM WOM WOM WOM

...TRANSFORMING TO SERVICE MODE...

HUH?

ALL RIGHT!

THAT MEANS I CAN HAVE IT, RIGHT?! LUCKY ME!!

I WANT MONEY, WOMEN, WRISTWATCHES— EVERYTHING.

BUT I WANT IT AT ANY COST— EVEN MY LIFE.

SHF

FAP

IT'S ONLY NATURAL THAT THE ONE WITH THE STRONGEST DESIRE SHOULD GET IT, RIGHT?

YOUR CUSTOMER IS CONCERNED ABOUT YOUR WELFARE AND YOU'RE STEALING HER ORDER?!

HEY...!

YOU SAID YOU WOULDN'T WANT THAT WATCH IF I DIED GETTING IT FOR YOU, RIGHT?

WELL...

UH-HUH...

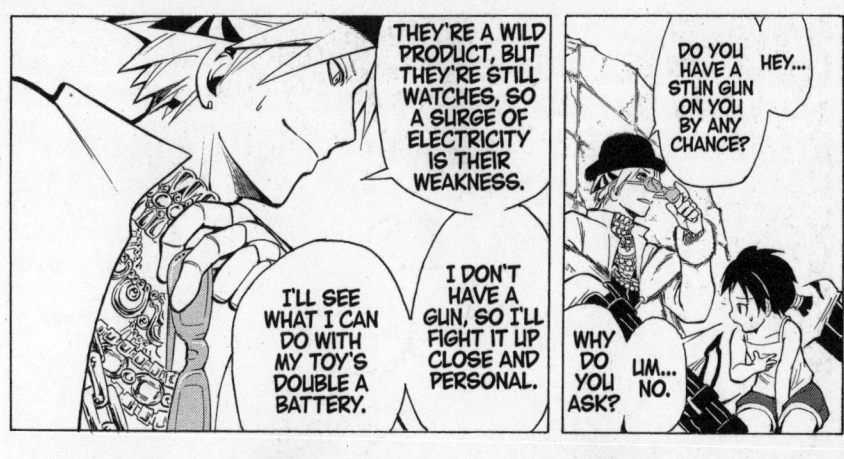

THEY'RE A WILD PRODUCT, BUT THEY'RE STILL WATCHES, SO A SURGE OF ELECTRICITY IS THEIR WEAKNESS.

I'LL SEE WHAT I CAN DO WITH MY TOY'S DOUBLE A BATTERY.

I DON'T HAVE A GUN, SO I'LL FIGHT IT UP CLOSE AND PERSONAL.

DO YOU HAVE A STUN GUN ON YOU BY ANY CHANCE?

HEY...

WHY DO YOU ASK?

UM... NO.

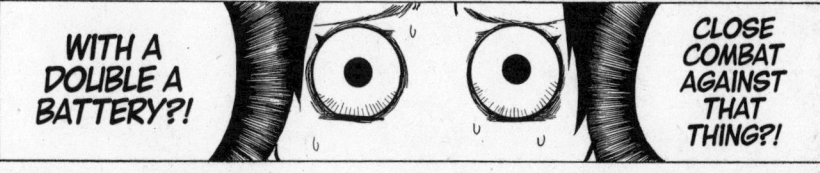

WITH A DOUBLE A BATTERY?!

CLOSE COMBAT AGAINST THAT THING?!

ALL I *WANTED* IS A WRISTWATCH.

IT'S NOT WORTH THE TROUBLE OF YOU DYING TO GET IT.

SO YOU'RE GIVING UP OUT OF CONCERN FOR MY WELL-BEING ...?

I SEE...

FORGET IT.

HEY...

I'LL JUST BUY...

...SOMETHING CHEAP ON THE OUTSIDE.

THE BIGGER THEIR BODIES, THE MORE NUTRITION THEY CAN PACK INTO THEIR FUNCTION AND DESIGN.

WHY? ?

THE BIGGER THE BETTER.

BIP BIP BIP

SURPRISINGLY, HERE AT THE WILD DEPARTMENT STORE, THE MANNEQUINS THEMSELVES CREATE THE PRODUCTS.

JUST LIKE AN OYSTER CREATES PEARLS.

LUBDUB

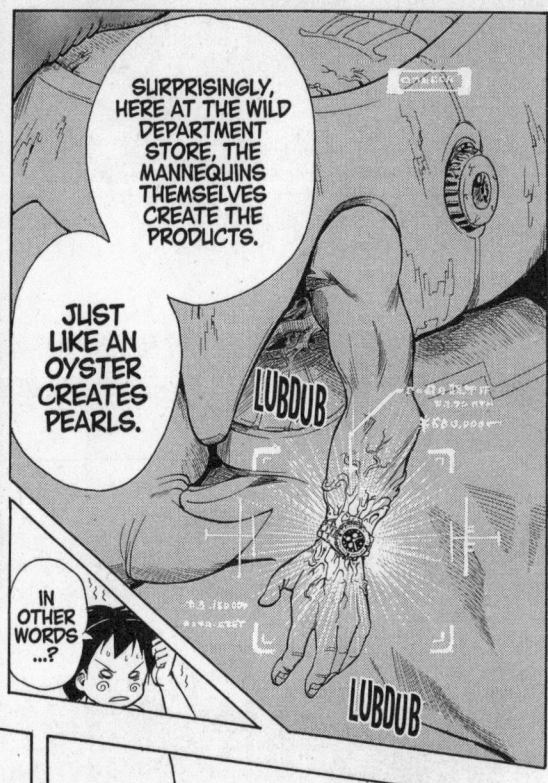

AS A RESULT, YOU GET HIGHER-QUALITY ITEMS.

IN OTHER WORDS...?

LUBDUB

HUGE, OF COURSE.

AND THE ONE WE'RE AFTER IS...?

THE BIGGEST AND STRONGEST MANNEQUINS SURVIVE TO GIVE BIRTH TO OFFSPRING— NEW MODELS.

IT'S THE FEATURED PRODUCT ON THIS FLOOR, SO...

SO THE PRODUCTS CONTINUE TO EVOLVE.

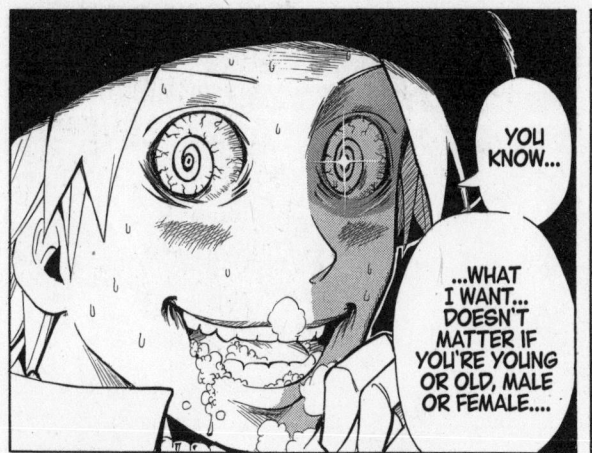

YOU KNOW...

...WHAT I WANT... DOESN'T MATTER IF YOU'RE YOUNG OR OLD, MALE OR FEMALE....

I DON'T HAVE ANY MONEY.

B-BUT...

DON'T WORRY. YOU DON'T HAVE TO PAY WITH MONEY.

HE'S A TOTAL CREEP!!

HOW ABOUT IT THEN ...?

WHAT DO YOU DESIRE?

TELL ME...

I GET THE FEELING HIS DESIRE IS MORE DANGEROUS THAN ANY OF THE WILD PRODUCTS...

SHOULD I REALLY STRIKE A DEAL WITH A GUY LIKE THIS?!

WILD PRODUCTS CAN ONLY BE ACQUIRED BY DEFEATING THEM.

I'LL BUY IT FOR YOU.

AFTER WHAT YOU'VE JUST OBSERVED, I'M SURE YOU'VE REALIZED YOU CAN'T MANAGE IT ON YOUR OWN.

WHAT?

I'LL BUY IT AND RESELL IT TO YOU.

TELL ME YOUR HEART'S DESIRE.

WILD MERCHANTS ...?

THAT'S WHAT WE DO.

THAT'S THE JOB OF US WILD MERCHANTS.

DOES IT SUIT ME?

Y-YOU DO?

HA HA HA.

I LIKE THE COLOR OF YOUR OUTFIT.

OH.

I'VE G-GOTTA HAVE IT!

TAKE IT OFF.

TRMBL

TRMBL

TRMBL

HFF HFF

YOU OUGHT TO BE GLAD IT'S ME WHO'S ASKING FOR IT.

COME ON...THINK OF IT AS MY REWARD FOR SAVING YOU!

THIS CREEP IS ATTACKING ME!!!

EEEEEEK, HE'S ROBBING ME!

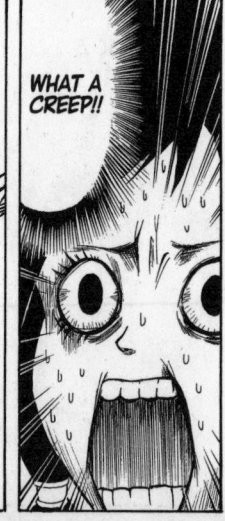

WHAT A CREEP!!

COUNTLESS WARS HAVE REDUCED ALL 23 WARDS OF TOKYO TO RUINS.

NOTHING TO EAT— OR WEAR.

IT'S AN IMPOVER- ISHED WORLD.

AND AT ITS CEN- TER...

...STANDS A DEPARTMENT STORE THAT SOARS INTO THE SKY.

RUMOR HAS IT YOU CAN OBTAIN ANYTHING YOU DESIRE HERE.

The following is a one-shot I created before *Assassination Classroom*.

Unfortunately, it didn't pass muster at the serialization meeting...but I started work on *Assassination Classroom* right after that, so I reused many of the character designs. In some ways, I think you could call this its antecedent, so I decided to introduce it here.

I also had some space left to introduce the unused rough drafts from *Time for the Yearbook*, the color illustration book published together with the final volume*. Please check that out too if you're interested.

*In Japan

GLEAM

Subtle advertisement

As the creator, I tried to tell them everything I knew so that we could create something the fans of the manga would enjoy watching. This intense communication turned out to be a wonderful experience for me.

People's expectations of media franchises have grown. Fortunately, as the creator of this series, I could not have asked for a better team to work with in terms of the movie and anime.

And so, I would like to bring this project to a close by saying that by blending the strengths of multiple platforms, I believe we have created a mutually beneficial relationship.

Thank you very much!

2016.7.4
松井優征

July 4, 2016
Yusei Matsui

Afterword ②
—*Assassination Classroom* Across Media Platforms—

When talking about *Assassination Classroom*, we can't ignore the media franchise aspect of the series.

I wanted the series, movie and anime to all end in the same way at roughly the same time, so from the moment the other projects were launched, I had to tell the others about the final chapter, and I kept in constant contact to maintain a unified theme and direction.

(I must apologize to the graphic novel team for the lateness of this volume due to juggling all these projects at once.)

The staff of the anime and the movie—the cast and producers—read between the lines of *Assassination Classroom* all the way through to the very end so as to fully bring out the charm of the series.

WE'RE ALL GROWING UP...

...AS WE WEAVE THE THREADS...

...OF OUR DEEPENING FRIENDSHIPS.

ASSASSINATION CLASSROOM 21 END OF EXTRA CLASSES

I BET WITH A TEACHER LIKE THAT...
...ALL HIS STUDENTS WILL FIND THEIR PLACE IN THE WORLD...
Izakaya Azusa
Pub
Fresh Sashimi 500 Yen
Chu-hi Beer 200 yen
Nagisa...
Nagisa...
NA-GISA!!
Z Z Z
Animal
Japanese

I ENJOYED SHARING SOME PLEASANT GROWN-UP TIME WITH YOU.

IT WAS NOTH-ING.

THANK YOU, MR. OCTOPUS...

SHORTLY AFTER THAT...

...MR. OCTOPUS STOPPED COMING TO OUR PUB.

Hey, Octopus! Get away from Ms. Azusa!! And put on your disguise!!

HE MUST BE BUSY DOING...

...THE ONE THING HE WANTS TO DO MOST OF ALL...

10 Training Sessions to Go into Space

THEN TAKE A GOOD LOOK NOW THAT YOU CAN SEE AGAIN.

I FIND IT HARD TO BELIEVE THERE IS ANYTHING OF VALUE IN ME.

...I JUST TRIED TO MAKE MONEY BY COMMITTING A SIN!

BUT...

Get in! Get in!

Ms. Azusa!

IF YOU WISH, YOU COULD CHOOSE ANY ONE OF THEM...OR JUST WRAP THEM ALL AROUND YOUR LITTLE FINGER.

LOOK AT ALL THESE MEN WHO SEE YOUR WORTH.

THAT'S MORE THAN ENOUGH TO MAKE ME GLAD TO BE ALIVE.

WHEN...

...I SEE THE LOOK ON ALL THEIR FACES.

I DON'T THINK I COULD BE THAT BAD...

I'VE LIVED MY LIFE TO THE FULLEST THERE.

I'LL HAVE NO REGRETS—NO MATTER WHAT SORT OF GRADUATION I FACE.

I WANT YOU TO LIVE YOUR LIFE TO THE FULLEST TOO, WITH HOTARU.

MY STUDENTS ARE PUTTING ALL THEIR EFFORT INTO MOVING FORWARD AS WELL.

PLEASE DON'T FORGET THAT YOUR LIFE HAS VALUE.

DID I LOOK LIKE I WAS HOLDING MYSELF BACK?

YOU SAW ME PLENTY OF TIMES BEFORE YESTERDAY, DIDN'T YOU?

PHEEEW

WINTER BREAK WILL BE OVER SOON...

...AND I WILL RETURN TO THE CLASSROOM.

HEH...

I SUP-POSE NOT.

YOU'VE BEEN QUITE THE FREE SPIRIT.

HIS REPRISAL AGAINST ASSASSINS...

...IS TO POLISH THEM!!

I MASTERED SURGERY WHILE WORKING AS A TEACHER...

...WHEN I TOOK OVER FOR HER.

BECAUSE I PROMISED A CERTAIN WOMAN THAT I WOULD PROTECT HER STUDENTS TO THE BITTER END...

...YOU SACRIFICE YOURSELF FOR THE SAKE OF EDUCATION.

YOU...

...

WHY ARE YOU SO...?

AREN'T YOU...

...SUP-PRESSING YOUR TRUE SELF...

...TO BEHAVE LIKE THE PERFECT TEACHER FOR EVERYONE ELSE'S BENEFIT?

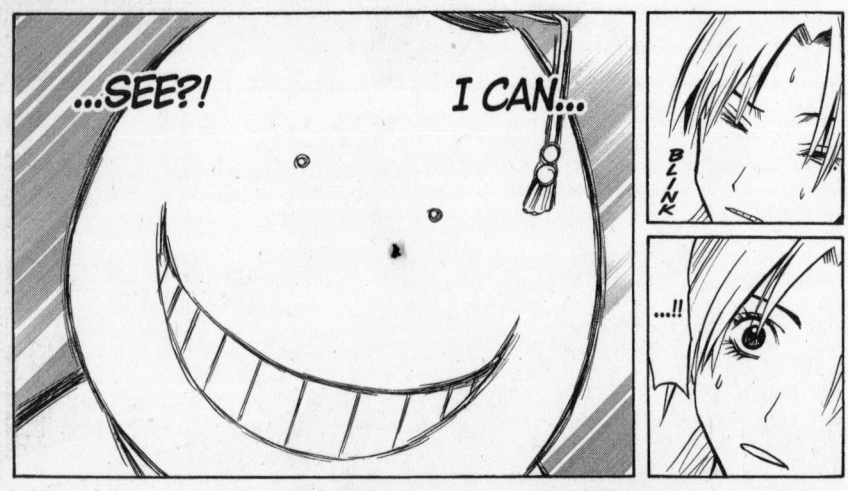

...SEE?!

I CAN...

BLINK

...!!

...AND DEVISED A PLAN TO REMOVE THE TUMOR.

I TOOK THE LIBERTY OF SCANNING YOUR BRAIN WHEN YOU HUGGED ME...

GRRRIN

AFTER SOME OBSERVATION, I COULD TELL THAT YOU HAD A BRAIN TUMOR.

HE, HOTARU AND YOU—THE THREE OF YOU...

...ARE ALL SELF-SACRIFICING PEOPLE WHO PLACE OTHERS BEFORE THEMSELVES.

MY STUDENT WHO TRIED TO SELF-DESTRUCT...

...IS A LOT LIKE HOTARU.

...SHE WOULD LEARN FROM HER MOTHER TO DO THE SAME THING FOR SOMEONE ELSE SOMEDAY.

SHE WOULD GROW UP TO BE A WOMAN PREPARED TO SACRIFICE HER LIFE FOR SOMEONE ELSE WITHOUT A SECOND THOUGHT.

IF YOU SACRIFICED YOURSELF FOR YOUR DAUGHTER HOTARU...

SLLLOOP

AND THAT...

...IS PEDAGOGICALLY UNACCEPTABLE!

!!

YOU HAVE THE RIGHT TO PUNISH ME AS YOU SEE FIT.

I DID WRONG.

YES...

ALL RIGHT...

YOU MAY FEEL A LITTLE PAIN...

I DON'T HAVE TIME TO BE GENTLE.

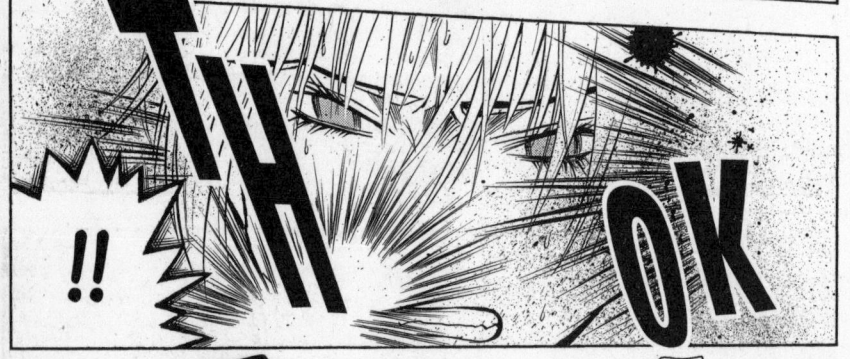

!!

OK

AIEEEE ...!!

ARRGH ...!!

THE BOUNTY OR THE LIFE INSURANCE POLICY.

THERE WAS A GOOD CHANCE ONE OF THOSE TWO WOULD PAY OFF.

THE GOVERNMENT WOULD MAKE ITS MOVE IF IT FOUND OUT THIS INCIDENT INVOLVED A NATIONAL SECRET— I.E., ME.

OTHERWISE, NO ONE WOULD EVER BELIEVE THAT A BLIND WOMAN HAD BLOWN HERSELF UP.

GR

HOW— EVER...

AB

SKWEEZ

SKWEEZ

SKWEEZ

ARE YOU SURE YOU'RE PREPARED TO FACE THE CONSEQUENCES?

...SINCE YOU JUST TRIED TO KILL ME, THAT MAKES YOU AN ASSASSIN YOURSELF!

SKWEEZ

SKWEEZ

AS LONG AS I BEQUEATH HER A LITTLE MONEY...

...SHE'LL BE ABLE TO MAKE A LIVING FOR HERSELF AND SURVIVE.

HOTARU...

...HAS GROWN UP A LOT RECENTLY.

I EVEN LEFT A LETTER ON MY DESK...

...HINTING THAT I KNEW ABOUT THE BOUNTY.

...AND STOLE MR. MARIO'S BOMB.

THAT'S WHY...

...I SIGNED UP FOR THE LIFE INSURANCE PLAN THAT LOAN SHARK SUGGESTED...

...AND IF I DIDN'T COME TO HELP YOU, YOU WOULD SELF-DESTRUCT WITH THE LOAN SHARKS.

IF I CAME TO HELP YOU, YOU WOULD KILL ME...

YOU DEVISED A FINE PLAN WITH A VERY GOOD CHANCE OF SUCCESS.

...I HAVE THREE YEARS LEFT...AT MOST.

I'VE BEEN TOLD THAT...

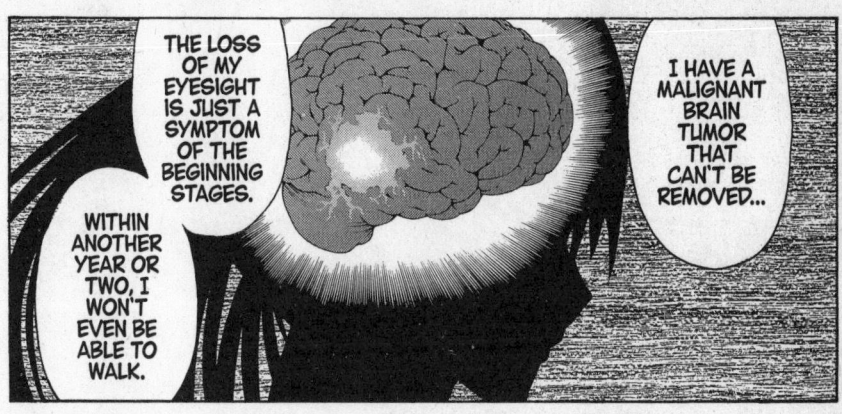

THE LOSS OF MY EYESIGHT IS JUST A SYMPTOM OF THE BEGINNING STAGES.

WITHIN ANOTHER YEAR OR TWO, I WON'T EVEN BE ABLE TO WALK.

I HAVE A MALIGNANT BRAIN TUMOR THAT CAN'T BE REMOVED...

IT WAS OBVIOUS THEY WEREN'T PRACTICING A PLAY.

YES.

...YOU HEARD ABOUT ME FROM THOSE GUYS, RIGHT?

AND THEN...

I DON'T HAVE MONEY FOR THE TREATMENT TO SAVE ME. AFTER ALL, I'M ALREADY UP TO MY NECK IN DEBT.

WHEN I DIE, HOTARU WILL BE DESTITUTE!

SKWEE

SKWEE

SHPRITZ

RUB

RUB

RUB

I WOULDN'T HAVE BEEN ABLE TO RESPOND SO QUICKLY...

...IF I HAD BEEN CAUGHT BY SURPRISE THOUGH...

...FAST, BUT...I NEVER DREAMED YOU WERE **THIS** FAST!

I HEARD THAT Y-YOU WERE...

...SO AS TO LURE YOU INTO EXECUTING YOUR ASSASSINATION PLAN WHEN WE WERE ALONE.

I HAD THE OTHERS GO ON AHEAD...

FROM THE MOMENT WHEN...

...I FIRST ENTERED YOUR PUB.

HOW LONG HAVE YOU KNOWN...?

...

FSHUuuu

...!!

SHWISH

SHWISH

KRAKL KRAKL

KLINK

SHWI

SHWI

TOO BAD FOR YOU THAT...

...MY TENTACLES ARE SPEEDIER THAN ANY EXPLODING BOMB!

HUH ...?

I'M SURE I JUST SELF-DESTRUCTED !!

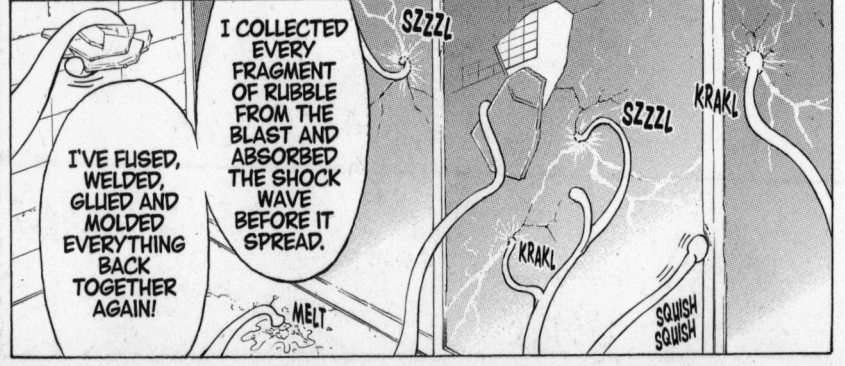

I'VE FUSED, WELDED, GLUED AND MOLDED EVERYTHING BACK TOGETHER AGAIN!

I COLLECTED EVERY FRAGMENT OF RUBBLE FROM THE BLAST AND ABSORBED THE SHOCK WAVE BEFORE IT SPREAD.

SZZZL

SZZZL

KRAKL

KRAKL

MELT

SQUISH SQUISH

KRAKABOOOOM

CATCHA
CATCHA
CATCHA
CATCHA
CATCHA
CATCHA
CATCHA
CATCH
CATCH
KLATTER
FWAPPA
FWAPPA
PFFT
PFFT
PFFT
CATCHA
FWAPPA
CATCH
CATCH
CATCH
CATCH
FWAPPA
FWAPPA
CATCH
GATHER
GATHER
CATCH
CATCH
FWAPPA
FWAPPA

Assassination Classroom

EXTRA CLASS #4 TIME TO SAY THANK YOU

GET A GRIP! WE'RE STILL ON ENEMY TURF!

HE DIDN'T LIFT A TENTACLE! BUT NOW HE'S STEALING THE SHOW FROM US!

DAMN IT!

AND HE'S THE BEST "MAN" FOR THE JOB—TO PROTECT HER.

I'LL WATCH OVER MS. AZUSA AND MEET YOU IN FRONT.

TAKE HOTARU WITH YOU AND BRING THE CAR OVER TO THE FRONT ENTRANCE.

...HELP PEOPLE IN ORDINARY WAYS, HUH...?

TURNS OUT WE CAN STILL...

BUT...

YEAH...

IF THE FOUR OF US JOINED FORCES, JUST IMAGINE WHAT WE COULD ACCOMPLISH!!

MAYBE IT'S TIME...

...I START OVER AND LOOK FOR A NEW JOB...

HOTARU !!

MOTHER !!

HOW CAN I POSSIBLY THANK YOU...?

I'M SO GRATEFUL!!

THEY WOULDN'T DARE COME AFTER YOU AGAIN.

YOU'LL BOTH BE FINE NOW.

I'LL STAY WITH YOU ALL NIGHT IF YOU WANT.

OF COURSE.

E-EXCUSE... ...ME...

OH...

STAGGER

I FEEL SO WEAK NOW THAT IT'S ALL OVER...

MAY I REST HERE FOR A WHILE?

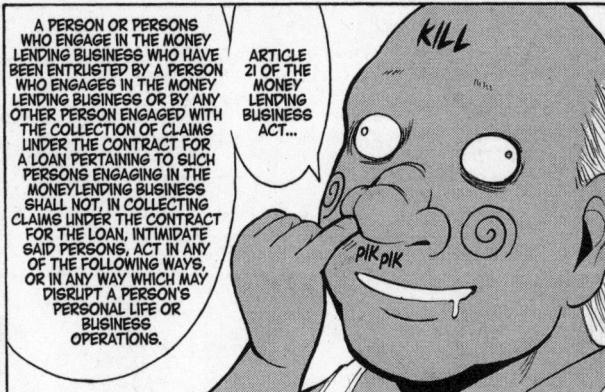

ARTICLE 21 OF THE MONEY LENDING BUSINESS ACT...

A PERSON OR PERSONS WHO ENGAGE IN THE MONEY LENDING BUSINESS WHO HAVE BEEN ENTRUSTED BY A PERSON WHO ENGAGES IN THE MONEY LENDING BUSINESS OR BY ANY OTHER PERSON ENGAGED WITH THE COLLECTION OF CLAIMS UNDER THE CONTRACT FOR A LOAN PERTAINING TO SUCH PERSONS ENGAGING IN THE MONEYLENDING BUSINESS SHALL NOT, IN COLLECTING CLAIMS UNDER THE CONTRACT FOR THE LOAN, INTIMIDATE SAID PERSONS, ACT IN ANY OF THE FOLLOWING WAYS, OR IN ANY WAY WHICH MAY DISRUPT A PERSON'S PERSONAL LIFE OR BUSINESS OPERATIONS.

KILL

PIK PIK

THOSE DAYS ARE IN THE PAST.

Y-YOU'RE ...

...A LAWYER?!

PLUS, RUNNING A LOAN COMPANY WITHOUT A PROPER LANDLINE PHONE BREACHES ARTICLE 47, PARAGRAPH 2, OF THE MONEYLENDING BUSINESS ACT, SO THE PENAL CODE WOULD SENTENCE YOU FOR KIDNAPPING FOR PROFIT, CONFINEMENT AND EXTORTION. IT DOESN'T MATTER IF YOU'VE GOT THE YAKUZA BEHIND YOU. ONCE WE GO TO TRIAL, YOU'RE THE ONE WHO'LL TAKE THE FALL FOR THIS.

ALSO, IN SIMPLE TERMS...YOUR INFLATED INTEREST RATE WOULD BE OVERRULED BY ARTICLE 1 OF THE INTEREST RATE RESTRICTION ACT, AND YOU WOULD BE EITHER IMPRISONED, FINED OR BOTH BECAUSE YOU HAVE BREACHED ARTICLE 5 OF THE ACT OF REGULATING THE RECEIPT OF CONTRIBUTIONS AND RECEIPT OF DEPOSITS AND INTEREST RATES. IN ADDITION, YOU ARE UNREGISTERED, WHICH BREACHES ARTICLE 11 OF THE MONEYLENDING BUSINESS ACT.

KILL

BUT I HAD A RIVAL WHO WAS AN EXPERT IN THIS BRANCH OF LAW AND PROSECUTION.

A LOT HAS TRANSPIRED BETWEEN US, BUT I CAN ALWAYS CALL THIS RIVAL TO LOOK INTO THE MATTER IF YOU LIKE...

ROLL

ROLL

YOU USED TO BE A WHAT?!

FUTOSHI...

SHE HIRED THUGS SO SHE COULD RENEGE ON HER DEBT, HUH?

I SEE.

TCH...

ACCIDENTAL DEATHS...

A FIRE AT THE PUB...

THERE ARE PLENTY OF OTHER WAYS TO GET BACK AT HER.

THE YAKUZA CLAN THAT BACKS US WILL NEVER ALLOW YOU TO WIN THIS.

FINE. SHOW US WHAT YOU'VE GOT.

I EXPLAINED THE RISKS AND THE REPAYMENT DEADLINES...

...AND SHE SIGNED AND SEALED IT OF HER OWN FREE WILL.

MOST OF ALL, THOUGH...

...I HAVE A LEGITIMATE LOAN CONTRACT WITH HER.

THE INTEREST RATE AND YOUR PAYMENT TERMS...? THEY'RE ALL ILLEGAL.

ACTUALLY... NO.

I'M SURE THEY'LL BEGIN TO WALK A NEW PATH THEMSELVES SOMEDAY.

MY RIVALS ARE GROWN-UPS WITH OPTIONS AND CHOICES AS WELL.

ACK...

HAND MS. AZUSA OVER!

I BET YOU TRICKED HER INTO TAKING ON TOO MUCH DEBT IN THE FIRST PLACE!

WHO...

...ARE Y-YOU GUYS?!

ALL OF YOU ...?!

....!

IT WAS ONLY NATURAL FOR ME TO RESEARCH MY MOST TALENTED BUSINESS RIVALS.

I, TOO, WAS IN THE SAME BUSINESS AS THEM ONCE.

I FOUND A JOB THAT INTERESTS ME EVEN MORE.

SIMPLE...

WHY DID YOU QUIT THAT JOB, MR. OCTOPUS?

PAT

...SACRIFICING ANYTHING AND EVERYTHING.

A WONDERFUL JOB FOR WHICH IT IS WORTH...

CHANTA WAS A SKILLED TECHNICIAN AT A SECURITY COMPANY.

MARIO WAS A BODYGUARD WHO PROTECTED ELITE CLIENTS.

...DRAGGED INTO SCANDALS THAT RESULTED IN THEM LOSING THEIR PLACE IN SOCIETY.

THEY WERE ALL...

AND THUS FATE LED THEM TO THEIR CURRENT LINE OF BUSINESS.

YOU'RE NOT FRIENDS.

HOW COME YOU KNOW SO MUCH ABOUT THEM, MR. OCTOPUS?

...COMPLI-CATED PASTS.

I GUESS A LOT OF GROWN-UPS HAVE...

BUT IT HASN'T ALWAYS BEEN LIKE THIS...

TMP

TMP

...THE H-HELL ARE YOU?!

WHO...

THUD

ZWISH

TH

CHOP

OK

IN THE OLD DAYS, WE, TOO, WERE LEGIT...

WE COULD JUST USE BRUTE FORCE TO GET THROUGH...

...BUT THAT'S MORE LIKELY TO ALERT SECURITY AND GIVE THEM TIME TO ESCAPE.

AUTO-MATIC LOCKS CAN BE QUITE TROUBLE-SOME.

BIP BOOP BAP

BIP BEEP BIP BIP

I CAN USE THE MASTER KEY I DEVELOPED TO OPEN IT.

BIIP BIP

SUCCESS

...THE IC CHIP SECURING THIS CONDO IS PRETTY SIMPLE TO DISABLE.

LUCKILY...

BUT...

...PLEASE RESOLVE THIS IN A WAY THAT WON'T... *DISILLUSION* HOTARU.

?

EASY FOR YOU TO SAY...

TCH...

WE'RE GONNA BREAK IN. YOU STAY HERE WITH HOTARU.

HEY, OCTO-PUS...

VERY WELL.

BUT...

...HE WAS FORCED TO TAKE FULL RESPONSIBILITY FOR THE CRASH OF A JUMBO JET...

...AND HAD TO GIVE UP HIS CAREER.

SEEKER WAS ONCE A SKILLED AIR TRAFFIC CONTROLLER.

Psst Psst

...HE CAME UP WITH A SYSTEM TO PINPOINT THE COORDINATES OF ANY TARGET IN THE WORLD.

...AND USING THE KNOWLEDGE HE'D ACQUIRED FROM HIS PREVIOUS JOB...

AFTER THAT, HE STUDIED DILIGENTLY...

SO IN ORDER TO MAKE A LIVING...

...HE MAKES USE OF HIS UNIQUE SKILLS IN A DIFFERENT "CAREER" AT THE MOMENT.

...IT'S IMPOSSIBLE FOR HIM TO REGAIN THE TRUST HE LOST.

UNFORTUNATELY...

TARGET

RMBL RMBL RMBL RMBL RMBL RMBL

EXTRA CLASS #3 | TIME TO REVEAL IDENTITIES

WELL, THERE WAS THE PHONE LOG AT THE PUB...

AND I HACKED THE SURVEILLANCE CAMERA IN THIS AREA.

BESIDES THAT, I DREW ON MY PERSONAL NETWORK, MADE SOME CALCULATIONS AND RELIED ON MY EXTENSIVE EXPERIENCE.

A LOAN SHARK'S OFFICE WITH NO CLEAR ADDRESS OR SIGN...

I'M AMAZED AT HOW QUICKLY YOU FOUND IT!

IT WAS A MILLION TIMES EASIER THAN FINDING THE OCTOPUS'S HIDEOUT, ANYWAY...

I'LL GO TOO!

I'll find them if it's the last thing I do...

Who are these people?!

HO-TARU...

SHE'S MY WHOLE WORLD!

I'M GOING TO GET MY MOTHER BACK!

ZLOOP

Extra Class #3 | Time to Reveal Identities

GRIN

AND IF...

...ANYTHING WERE TO HAPPEN TO HER...

...YOU WOULDN'T HAVE A PLACE TO GATHER ANYMORE.

The Truth Revealed!
The Top 3 Really Close Assassination Attempts

 ## Summer-Break Assassination

Even I have a brain inside my head, so having two bullets fly at me from my blind spot was the most dangerous moment of all. If I had been 0.08 seconds slower at changing into my Absolute Defense Form, there would have been one heaven-sent octopus in the sea. It was a wonderful assassination with the entire class working together.

 ## Kayano's Tentacle Assassination

I escaped so narrowly that I was shivering in my bath after I got home, muttering with my teeth chattering, "Pheeeeew...that was too close for comfort!" Kayano skillfully cornered me and Nagisa skillfully stopped her. It was the moment when you both perfected your art as assassins.

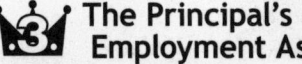 ## The Principal's Renewal-of-Employment Assassination

At a glance, it might seem like I received my biggest injury yet, but I knew where the attack was coming from, so I tensed up my entire body to prevent the pellets from penetrating deeply into me. And I trusted Principal Asano as an educator, so I knew that the explosion wouldn't be so strong as to injure any of the students.

...YOU NEED TO PROTECT YOUR REPUTATION WITH YOUR STUDENTS NO MATTER WHAT, DON'T YOU?

AS A TEACHER...

GRIN

WE ASSASSINS HAVE THINGS WE WANT TO PROTECT TOO, YOU KNOW!

SKWK

THIS IS *OUR* JOINT, AND WE'RE GONNA PROTECT IT *OURSELVES*!

STAND ASIDE AND WATCH, MR. TARGET...

KILL

SOUNDS LIKE A CASE FOR ME.

KILL

HMPH

I COULD SOLVE THIS PROBLEM IN HALF AN HOUR.

YOU'RE ALL AWARE OF WHAT I'M CAPABLE OF, AREN'T YOU?

IF YOU BUTT IN, I'M GONNA SHOW THESE PICTURES TO YOUR STUDENTS!

YOU STAY OUT OF THIS!

AIYEEE!!

FWAPP

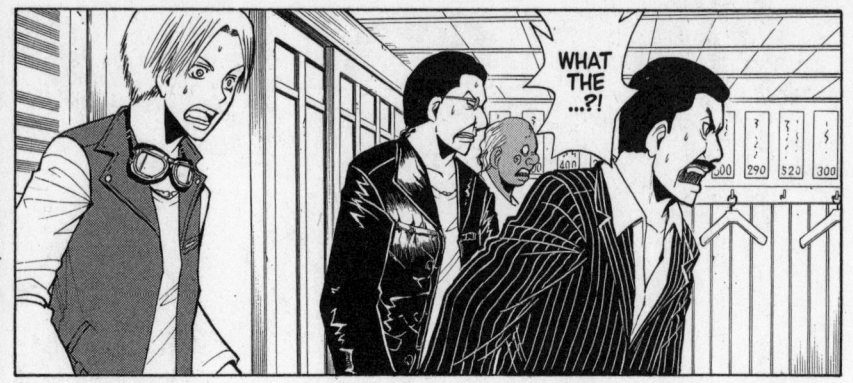

KILL

THIS AIN'T GOOD...

MS. AZUSA IS IN *BIG* TROUBLE!

BUT HOW CAN WE HELP ...?

I KNEW THIS PLACE WASN'T DOING TOO GOOD, BUT...

...FOR REAL ?!

...I HAD NO IDEA SHE WAS IN SUCH DEBT!

...NOTHING WE CAN DO...

THERE'S ...

KR

KRASH

OH, HEY THERE, HOTARU...

DON'T WORRY.

YOUR MOTHER'S JUST TAKING ON A NEW JOB.

YANK

ASH

Ho... ta-ru...

YOU COULD PAY HER DEBT BACK FASTER THAT WAY...

Heh heh heh heh heh...

MAYBE YOU'D LIKE TO HELP YOUR MOM WITH HER WORK?

Z HWOOP

...!!

WE'LL DISCUSS YOUR RE-PAYMENT PLAN AT MY OFFICE.

LET'S GO.

WHAT...?!

WHERE...?!

GRAB

EVEN BETTER, YOU'RE BLIND.

POLITICIANS AND CEOS WILL PAY BIG BUCKS FOR YOU TO PRESERVE THEIR ANONYMITY.

IT'S A SHAME TO WASTE ALL THAT IN A DINGY DIVE LIKE THIS.

WITH YOUR LOOKS AND YOUR BOD...

HO-TARU!!

!

MOM?!

IT'S NOTHING.

THANK YOU FOR HELPING US OUT.

THE DEBT YOUR DECEASED HUSBAND OWES US...

...HAS GROWN TO TEN MILLION.

AT THIS RATE, IT LOOKS LIKE THERE'S NO WAY YOU'RE GOING TO BE ABLE TO PAY WHAT YOU OWE.

...!!

M-MR. ...

...SEN-GOKU!

UH-HUH.

APPARENTLY YOU HAVEN'T FORGOTTEN YOUR DEAR CREDITOR'S VOICE.

KLATTA

Pub

Izakaya Azusa

... HERE. UM, THE GLASSES FOR THE SAKE GO...

I'M VERY GRATEFUL THAT...

...HOTARU IS SO MATURE AND HELPFUL.

ALL THE GLASSES ARE BACK WHERE THEY BELONG.

SHE'S BEEN PITCHING IN WITH THE CLEANING TOO THESE DAYS.

YOU MUST BE DELIVERING THE LIQUOR.

OH, ARE YOU FROM OUR SUPPLIER?

STAGGER

ZLOOP

...

KILL

...ANY OF US COULD PROVIDE FOR THOSE TWO AND MAKE THEM HAPPY?

BUT DO YOU REALLY THINK...

THERE'S NO WAY SHE'LL FALL FOR THAT OCTOPUS!

NAH...

WE CAN'T BE PROUD OF WHAT WE DO FOR A LIVING.

...

Beer Shochu

Hot Sake

WE MET HER FIRST!

DAMN HIM...

YOU DO...?

WE'VE GOT AN EARLY DAY TOMOR-ROW.

CHECK, PLEASE...

MS. AZU-SA!

...

GOOD NIGHT.

IT'S COLD OUT THERE! STAY WARM!

AND HOTARU IS SUCH A GOOD GIRL.

I WISH THEY WERE MY FAMILY...

MS. AZUSA...

...IS SO PRETTY...

GOOD NIGHT.

YEAH...

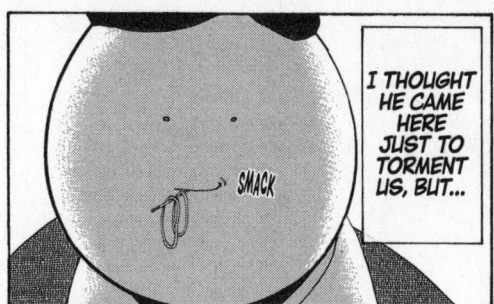

I THOUGHT HE CAME HERE JUST TO TORMENT US, BUT...

SMACK

I CAN'T BELIEVE THIS GUY...

HUUUUG...

HUG

HERE YOU GO...

WELL, LIKE I PROM-ISED...

MR. OCTOPUS WON BY A LANDSLIDE!

THIS IS BORING. HE'S TOO GOOD.

GRIN

...AFTER MS. AZUSA TOO?!

WRGGL.

IS THE OCTOPUS...

WRGGL.

WRGGL.

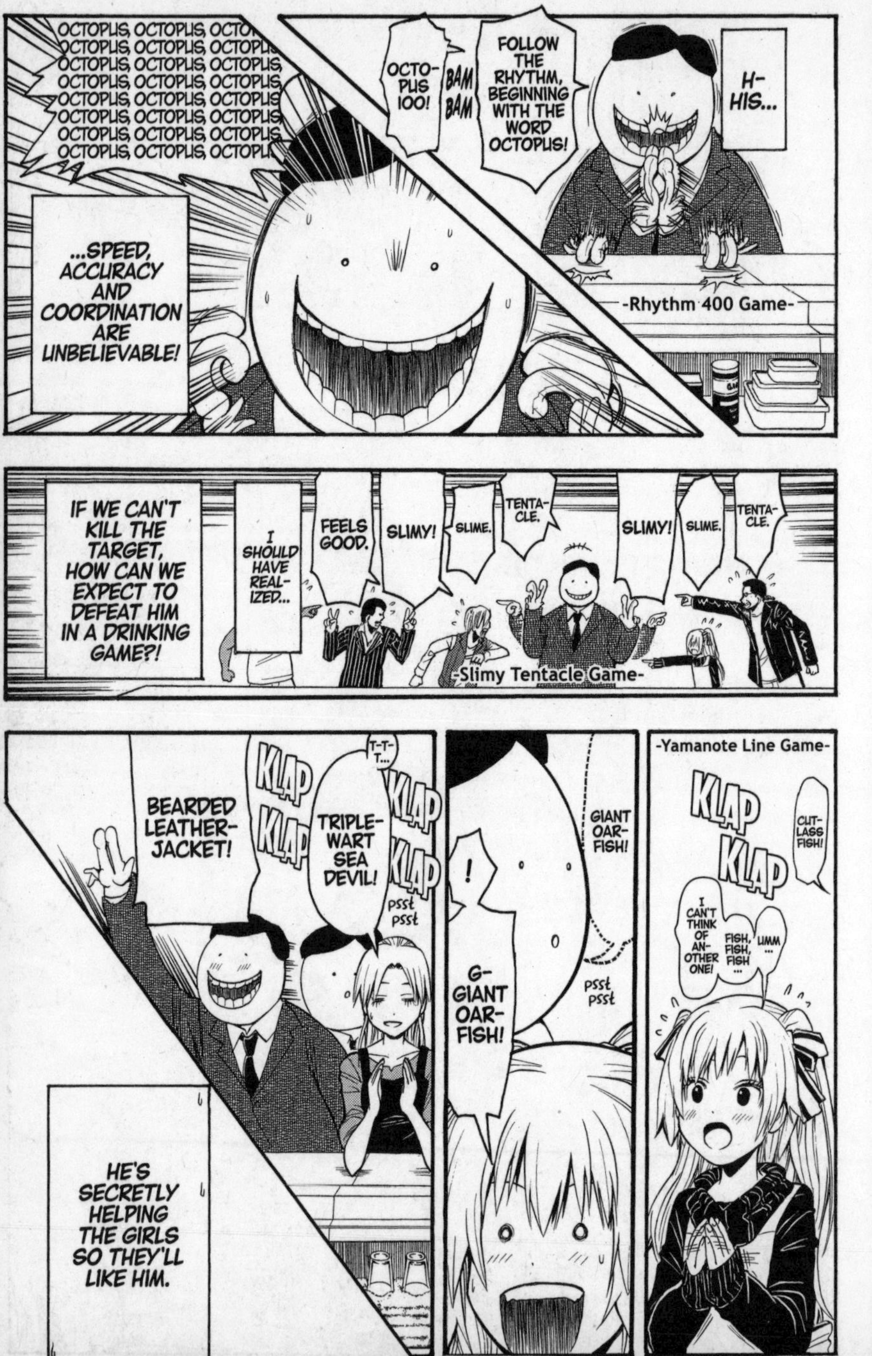

OCTOPUS, OCTOPUS, OCTOP...

OCTO-PUS 100!

BAM BAM

FOLLOW THE RHYTHM, BEGINNING WITH THE WORD OCTOPUS!

H-HIS...

-Rhythm 400 Game-

...SPEED, ACCURACY AND COORDINATION ARE UNBELIEVABLE!

IF WE CAN'T KILL THE TARGET, HOW CAN WE EXPECT TO DEFEAT HIM IN A DRINKING GAME?!

I SHOULD HAVE REALIZED...

FEELS GOOD.

SLIMY!

SLIME.

TENTA-CLE.

SLIMY!

SLIME.

TENTA-CLE.

-Slimy Tentacle Game-

BEARDED LEATHER-JACKET!

KLAP KLAP

T-T-T...

KLAP KLAP

TRIPLE-WART SEA DEVIL!

PSST PSST

HE'S SECRETLY HELPING THE GIRLS SO THEY'LL LIKE HIM.

!

G-GIANT OAR-FISH!

GIANT OAR-FISH!

PSST PSST

-Yamanote Line Game-

KLAP KLAP

CUT-LASS FISH!

I CAN'T THINK OF AN-OTHER ONE!

FISH, FISH, FISH...

UMM ...

HOW ABOUT I GIVE HIM A *BIG HUG*?!

ALL WE'VE GOT IS A MIDDLE-AGED WOMAN AND AN ELEMENTARY SCHOOL STUDENT... BUT THAT'S BETTER THAN NOTHING.

THE PERSON WHO GETS THE HIGHEST SCORE WINS A...LET'S SEE...

WE ARE TRULY IN THE PRESENCE OF TWO ANGELS...

KILL

WAIT...

YOU'RE JOINING IN, HOTARU?!

I'M THE DAUGHTER OF A PUB OWNER. WHY DOES IT SURPRISE YOU THAT I KNOW HOW TO PLAY MIXER GAMES?

AS LONG AS YOU PLAY NON-ALCOHOLIC GAMES.

NO, I AM!

I'M GONNA WIN MS. AZUSA'S HUG!

YEAH!

OKAY! LET'S DO IT, GUYS!

YOU DON'T HOLD BACK WHEN YOUR STUDENTS AREN'T AROUND, DO YOU?!

LET'S HAVE A MIXER!

GUYS WHO FANTASIZE ABOUT UNIVERSITY STUDENTS TEND TO BE MIDDLE-AGED OLD FARTS, YOU KNOW.

YOU SURE ARE OBSESSED WITH UNIVERSITY STUDENTS.

...WITH UNIVERSITY WOMEN.

...AND PLAY DRINKING GAMES TO MAKE FRIENDS...

I WANT TO JOIN SILLY CLUB ACTIVITIES...

WITH A BOOBALICIOUS UNIVERSITY STUDENT, FOR EXAMPLE...

...POPULAR WITH THE LADIES.

I JUST WANT TO BE...

HUG

Koro Sensei's Adult Weakness 10
He's a middle-aged cliché.

...WHY DON'T YOU DO IT HERE?

THEN...

YOU CAN HOLD A MAKE-BELIEVE MIXER!

WHAT?!

HELL NO!

...TOGETHER! LET'S GO TO A MIXER...

COME ON!

I CAN'T IMAGINE HITTING ON GIRLS WITH YOU IN PUBLIC!

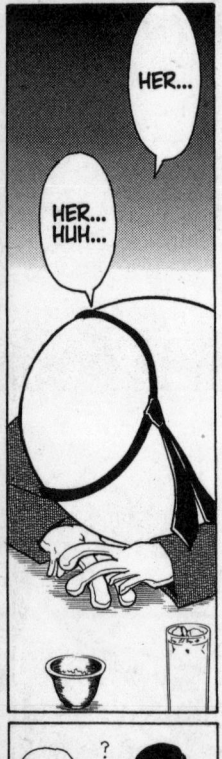

HE'S WIDE OPEN, DAMMIT!

Koro Sensei's Adult Weakness 8
Can't hold his liquor (obviously).

CAN'T... DRINK ANY... MORE...

HICCUP!

FWWOP

WHAT ARE THEY **DOING**?!

THEIR SPECIAL EFFECTS MAKEUP IS **AMAZING**.

RE-HEARSING THEIR PLAY AS USUAL.

HE STILL MANAGED TO DODGE OUR ATTACK, EVEN THOUGH HE'S WASTED!

SWISH

YOU JUST TOOK ONE SIP OF YOUR CASSIS AND ORANGE! HOW COME YOU'RE DEAD DRUNK ALREADY?!

BLEARRGH

Barf Bag

THANK YOU VERY MUCH, HOTARU.

HERE'S YOUR CASSIS AND ORANGE, MR. OCTOPUS.

WE'RE PROBABLY THE ONLY ONES LEFT WHO ARE STILL AFTER HIM.

...GAVE UP BEFORE WINTER SET IN.

ALL THE OTHER ASSASSINS...

B-B-M-P

B-B-M-P

Futoshi
Booger Specialist

Chanta
Lock-Picking Specialist

Seeker
Expert Tracker

Mario
Knife and Gun Specialist

IF HE LETS HIS GUARD DOWN, WE'LL KILL HIM!

EVEN NOW...

B-B-M-P

LICK

IF THEY OVERHEAR US TALKING ABOUT ASSASSINATING THE OCTOPUS, WE CAN JUST PRETEND WE'RE REHEARSING A PLAY.

THIS PUB IS THE PERFECT MEETING PLACE FOR US BECAUSE THE OWNER IS BLIND AND HER SERVER IS HER DAUGHTER— A CLUELESS ELEMENTARY SCHOOL STUDENT.

...OUR MIND-SET HAS CHANGED.

...SINCE WE'VE BEEN MEETING HERE SO OFTEN TO PLAN OUR ASSASSINA-TION AND KEEP UP OUR SPIRITS...

BUT...

Extra Class #2 Time to Go to the Izakaya

...AN OASIS STAFFED BY TWO ANGELS...

...MS. AZUSA AND HOTARU!

THIS PLACE HAS BECOME...

WHAT WOULD YOU LIKE TO DRINK...

...MR. OCTO-PUS?

The Truth Revealed! The Secret of Mach 20!

My maximum speed of Mach 20 is not as universal as you might think. The only place I can accelerate to a speed of Mach 20 is at high altitude or above the sea. In smaller areas with lots of obstacles, I wouldn't be able to make quick enough turns and my motion perception wouldn't keep up with my velocity.

Therefore, in other places, I usually move at subsonic speeds only up to Mach 3.

So, actually, being shot by anti-me BBs from close range was far more threatening than you could imagine. You can easily dodge a car driving toward you at 31 mph from a great distance, but if a professional boxer were to punch you at 31 mph from up close, you'd never be able to dodge the blow.

And so, although you probably never noticed it, I barely managed to evade your assassination attempts in the small space of the classroom and amongst the trees of the forest. As a result, your assassination attempts were quite exhilarating. And at the same time, I had the pleasure of observing your skills improve from day to day!

NOD

HE'S A TEACHER.

HE TOLD ME I REMIND HIM OF ONE OF HIS STUDENTS.

...IS A SHORT WINTER TALE...

AND THAT...

...ABOUT US AND A WARM GROUP OF FRIENDS.

Izakaya Azusa

YOU SEEM LIKE SUCH GOOD FRIENDS.

I WISH I COULD SEE...

...WHAT MR. OCTOPUS, THE MAIN CHARACTER OF YOUR PLAY, LOOKS LIKE.

KILL

YOU DON'T NEED TO BOTHER WITH A MONSTER LIKE HIM, MS. AZUSA!

NO NO NO!

KILL

I'M THE ONE WHO'S GONG TO GET THE BOUNTY SO I CAN ASK MS. AZUSA OUT.

YOU WON'T PULL ONE OVER ON ME.

YOU BETTER NOT GET THE JUMP ON ME.

WE COULD ASSAS- SINATE HIM IF WE WORKED TOGETHER ...

TCH. WE FAILED AGAIN.

HOW ARE WE GOING TO KILL THAT OCTOPUS ?!

AND SO HE GOT AWAY...

KLNK KLNK

KLNK

SPLISH

KILL

PICK PICK

WE DON'T ...

WHO THE HELL ARE YOU, ANYWAY?!

...WANT THAT!

IT'S ON ME.

KILL

ZWOOP

THEY HAVE TO FIND THOSE ANSWERS FOR THEMSELVES.

THAT'S THE ONE THING I CAN'T ASSIST THEM WITH.

BUT I WENT THROUGH SO MUCH TROUBLE TO FIND IT!

WHAT?!

HM...

NOW THEN...

GUESS I'LL LOUNGE AROUND A LITTLE LONGER AND THEN PACK UP AND MOVE MY HIDEOUT.

...

SQUSHY SQUSHY

WITH MY SPEED, I CAN RELOCATE IN A MATTER OF 30 MINUTES.

TOO BAD FOR YOU, HUH?

SAINT, MY FOOT!

YOU COLLECT PORN MAGAZINES OFF THE STREET NEAR THE SCHOOL TOO!

I HAVE THE RIGHT TO LET OFF A LITTLE STEAM EVERY NOW AND AGAIN!!

I'M AS VIRTUOUS AS A SAINT AT SCHOOL!

SNIFFLE

I NOTICE THEY HAVEN'T BEEN TRYING TO ASSASSINATE YOU LATELY...

...WHAT ARE YOUR STUDENTS UP TO NOW?

BY THE WAY...

BUT I TAKE MY HAT OFF TO YOU. YOU CERTAINLY ARE A SKILLED PROFESSIONAL ASSASSIN.

EVEN MY STUDENTS HAVEN'T HAVE BEEN ABLE TO LOCATE MY HIDEOUT.

Hmph.

THEY'RE TRYING TO SOLVE THEIR WINTER BREAK HOMEWORK PROBLEMS.

•••

STUDIO?!

AIIYEE!

YOU WEREN'T DOING ANYTHING CON- STRUCTIVE IN THERE!

I TAKE ONE DAY A MONTH TO COM- PLETELY SLACK OFF...

...IN A PLACE WHERE I WON'T SET A BAD EXAMPLE FOR MY STUDENTS!

YOOOOU... SAAAAW... MEEEE...

YOU SAW MY ADULT STUDIO!

SWISH

TCH

HE JUST SITS THERE AND STARES AT THEM. LIKE HE'S IN A STATE OF BLISS OR SOMETHING.

SOFT-CORE GIRLIE MAGS HE'S GATHERED FROM THE STREETS AND BACK ALLEYS OF THE WORLD!

YOU HAVEN'T DONE ANYTHING!

PHEEEW

I DID IT!

IS HE MEDITATING? IS THAT AN EXPRESSION OF ENLIGHTEN-MENT ON HIS FACE?

Koro Sensei's Adult Weakness 5
Collecting girlie mags replaced his goal of looking at them.

BIP

YOU WERE SUPPOSED TO CALL US AS SOON AS YOU FOUND HIM!

SO...WHAT DID YOU DO AFTER YOU CAUGHT HIM ON VIDEO?

HE IS ONE SERIOUS SLEAZEBAG.

I NEVER IMAGINED HE'D BE THIS MUCH WORSE OUTSIDE OF SCHOOL!

WELL, ABOUT THAT...

BIP

KILL

PICK PICK

Ahhhh...

CHAK

OTHER ROOM...?

HE WOKE UP AND HEADED FOR THE OTHER ROOM.

THE BEST IS YET TO COME...

SHAA

THIS ROOM IS THE MOST IMPORTANT ONE IN HIS HIDEOUT...

THIS IS THE BIGGEST SHOCK-ER OF ALL!

SHUNK

Y-YOU... ...MEAN...

...IT'S A ROOM FULL OF INTEL ABOUT US ASSASSINS?!

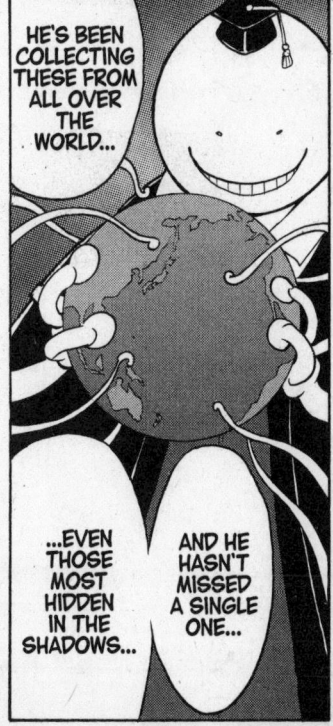

HE'S BEEN COLLECTING THESE FROM ALL OVER THE WORLD...

NOPE.

BUT GET A LOAD OF THIS!

HE KNOWS ALL THE ASSASSINA-TION PLANS OF THE WORLD'S ASSASSINS BEFORE THEY IMPLEMENT THEM...?!

...EVEN THOSE MOST HIDDEN IN THE SHADOWS...

AND HE HASN'T MISSED A SINGLE ONE...

SLAM

HE'S PANICKING BECAUSE HE LOST THE HORSE RACE.

HE DOESN'T REALIZE THAT HE CAN'T SCRATCH THE TICKET WITH HIS TENTACLE TIPS...

SLIME SLIP SLIME

SCRATCH

2 3
4 5

SLIME SLIP SLIME

SLIP SLIP

SLIP

SLIME

SLIME SLIME

SLIME SLIME SLIME

HE ONLY BOUGHT ONE TICKET THOUGH...

NEXT, HE TRIES TO GET A CONSOLATION PRIZE WITH A SCRATCH-OFF TICKET...

STARE

HE STAYED UNDER THERE FOR ABOUT THREE HOURS.

FWOOMF

IN THE END, HE LOST BOTH TIMES AND WENT AND SULKED INSIDE THE KOTATSU.

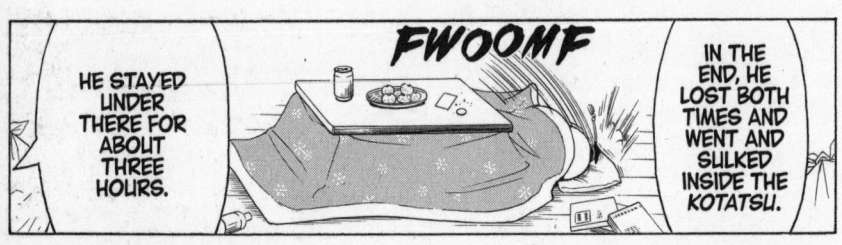

THAT'S TOTALLY THE LIFE OF A TOTAL LOSER!

WHIFE

GLOM

GLOM

TAP TAP

TO GET ICE CREAM FROM THE FREEZER, MANGA FROM THE SHELF AND MANDARIN ORANGES FROM THE ENTRANCE-WAY...

SWIPE

...HE JUST STRETCHED OUT HIS TENTACLES AND GRABBED THEM WITHOUT GETTING UP.

GLURP

TAP TAP

Koro Sensei's Adult Weakness 4
Slacker cephalopod.

THE BACK FIELD IS GRADUALLY CLOSING IN! TEKIRO-BRYAN IS RUSHING IN FROM THE OUTSIDE! MATSUKAZE-PANDORA ISN'T MADE HIS MOVE YET! IT'S GONNA IS KEEPING UP MIDDLE OF THE FIELD! LOOKS LIKE WE HAVE

C'MON ...!!

C'MON ...!!

OHHHH ...

YEAAH!

Month Cup
Horse Race

WHOA...

GAMBLING ...?

OH.

HE LOST THE RACE.

NOOOOOO!

C'MON, C'MON, C'MON, C'MON, C'MON, C'MO...

EVEN IF HE'D WON, HE'D ONLY HAVE MADE ABOUT A HUNDRED YEN WITH THAT STRATEGY!

Hanshin 12 Race Quinella ボックス BOX 2 3 7

HE ONLY BET 300 YEN ANYWAY. WHAT A CHEAPSKATE.

AND HE PLACED BOX BETS ON THE FAVORITE TO WIN.

Koro Sensei's Adult Weakness 3
Cheap gambler.

LOOKS LIKE HE WASHES AND REUSES DISPOSABLE CHOPSTICKS TOO...

MANDARIN ORANGE

LOOK AT THE RIDICULOUS AMOUNT OF EXTRA RED-PICKLED-GINGER PACKS HE TOOK FOR HIS TO-GO BEEF BOWL.

MAYBE HE DOESN'T MAKE ENOUGH MONEY FROM TEACHING?

MNCH MNCH

HOW HIGH CAN HIS LIVING EXPENSES BE?!

WELL, HE SPENDS A LOT OF MONEY ON HIS STUDENTS...

SO THEN, ALL OF A SUDDEN, HIS EYES ...

ZOING

...CHANGED. HE WAS LIKE A WILD CARNIVORE HUNTING AN HERBIVORE!

...HE'S A COMMON *THIEF!*

D-DON'T TELL ME...

ZLOOP

THERE AREN'T ANY SIGNS OF HIM MOON-LIGHTING.

I ASSUME THE SCHOOL IS HIS ONLY SOURCE OF INCOME.

Koro Sensei's
Adult Weakness 2
Lives in a pigsty

WHOA!

IT WAS A HOARDER'S DEN.

SHEESH...

SOME PEOPLE ALWAYS HAVE TO BUY THE LATEST CUP NOODLES...

I'VE NEVER SEEN THAT FLAVOR OF CUP NOODLES BEFORE.

LOOK AT ALL THOSE CRAPPY TOYS—THE TYPE SOLD AT THE CHECKOUT COUNTER!

...HE DOES WEAR DRAG EVERY NOW AND AGAIN.

YEAH, BUT...

INSIDE, HE'S BASICALLY JUST A MIDDLE-AGED DUDE.

WHAT DOES HE NEED WITH MAKE-UP?

WHAT KIND OF GROWN-UP CAN'T RESIST THOSE IMPULSE BUYS?

EVERY ONE ONE OF US ASSASSINS ...

...HAS GOTTEN CLEANED AND POLISHED BY HIM EVERY TIME WE'VE TANGLED WITH HIM SO FAR.

WELL ...?

WHAT'S IT LIKE ON THE INSIDE ?!

House-cleaner's Friend

far...a

SO I FIGURE HIS HIDE-OUT IS...

...RIDICULOUSLY CLEAN AND TIDY!

AM I RIGHT ?

ONE GUY HAD HIS ENTIRE HOUSE CLEANED FROM TOP TO BOTTOM. AND HIS HIDDEN PORN MAGS ALL NEATLY LAID OUT ON HIS DESK.

HE GAVE ME AN INTENSIVE HAIR-REMOVAL SESSION. MY UPPER ARM IS SILKY SMOOTH NOW.

But my hairy fore-arms were cool!

FWFF

TAP

...

D-DUM **D-DUM** **D-DUM** **D-DUM** **D-DUM** **D-DUM**

Koro Sensei's
Adult Weakness 1
Branded House.

IT STICKS OUT LIKE A SORE THUMB!

AND HE JUST WALTZES THROUGH THE FRONT ENTRANCE LIKE HE'S COMING HOME FROM WORK!

Phew. I'm so-o-o-o exhausted.

SKWEE

IT'S LOCATED IN THE MIDDLE OF A FIELD OF SNOW FAR FROM ANY HUMAN HABITATION...

...BUT I'VE NEVER SEEN SUCH A CONSPICUOUS SECRET LAIR IN MY LIFE!

SERVE IT QUICKLY BEFORE IT COOLS OFF.

ORDER UP, HOTARU.

Izakaya Azusa

Pub

Beer Shochu

Hot Sake Hoppy

MOTHER'S EYESIGHT IS DETERIORATING...

...SO I'VE BEEN HELPING HER OUT AT THE RESTAURANT.

WE GET A LOT OF ORDERS FOR...

...HOT SAKE AT THE END AND BEGINNING OF THE YEAR.

YAMMER

YAMMER

...ODD CUSTOMERS, THAT'S FOR SURE!

WE GET A LOT OF...

EXTRA CLASS #1 TIME TO COME HOME

The following four chapters were created after the series ended to support the newly released *Assassination Classroom: Graduation* movie and the second season of the *Assassination Classroom* anime. *Assassination Classroom* appears across several media platforms, so I wrote another afterword for these four chapters. Please take a look at the afterword at the end too if you have time.

He can get to Shonan where *that* shared house is apparently located in roughly eight seconds.	12 times faster than the Concorde.
He can get to Toho Cinemas Roppongi Hills in a matter of seconds.	Roughly 80 times faster than the maximum speed of the NINJA ZX-14R.
A troublesome teacher whose shenanigans at Mach 20 are nevertheless often spotted.	48 times faster than the Linear Chuo Shinkansen, which is currently recruiting test riders from ordinary citizens on the experimental line in Yamanashi Prefecture.
He can travel from Tokyo to the desert of Giza in roughly 25 minutes.	
	57.4 times faster than the frigate bird.
He would arrive in Kentucky in roughly 26 minutes.	240 times faster than a bonito swimming seriously.
Roughly 1,412 times faster than a pig.	153 times faster than the fastest pitch of handsome Takuya Asao.
Roughly 300 times faster than a gnu.	
It's not clear if he is 20 times faster than J's Mach Punch in the classic boys' manga *Sakigake Otokojuku*.	218 times faster than the oddly spelled Rapi:t, the red express train of Nankai Electric Railway.
470 times faster than a donkey.	0.85 times faster than first cosmic velocity.
He can travel to Tanegashima in two and a half minutes.	Roughly 60 times faster than the MTT Y2K, a motorbike with a jet engine.
44 times faster than the Transrapid train.	Roughly 87.3 times faster than Yamagata Shinkansen, Tsubasa, which has just been redesigned.
He can travel from Tokyo to Fushimi in Kyoto in roughly 55 seconds.	
Roughly 787 times faster than the 50-meter dash performed by Okoye from Kanto Ichi High School.	384 times faster than the Rhodesian ridgeback, otherwise known as the African lion hound.
Roughly 168 times faster than the 89 mph pitch Ichiro threw at his pitching debut in Major League Baseball.	480 times faster than a capybara.
	Roughly 91.3 times faster than the fastest serve recorded in tennis (held by Australia's Samuel Groth).
He can travel to Eden Park, where the international games of the New Zealand Originals rugby team are held, in roughly 22 minutes.	
	Roughly 342 times faster than an orca, the most powerful marine mammal.
Roughly 666 times faster than the "human locomotive" Jonah Lomu performing his 100-meter run.	He can travel from Tokyo to Rabat, the capital of Morocco, in roughly 29 minutes.
He can travel to Nagata-cho, Kagoshima, hometown of Tomoatsu Godai, in roughly two and a half minutes.	Roughly 218 times faster than the Indo-Pacific sailfish, the fastest fish of the marlin family, said to be the fastest of all swimmers.
It would take him 16 hours to travel in a straight line from the Earth to the moon.	He can travel from Tokyo to Manhattan in roughly 27 minutes.
He can travel from Osaka to North Kyushu in roughly 65 seconds.	Roughly 428.5 times faster than a Mediterranean flying fish.
Roughly 666 times faster than the swimming speed of a gentoo penguin.	He can arrive at Team Syachihoko's Nagoya headquarters in roughly 40 seconds.
Roughly 888 times faster than a honeybee.	He can migrate to Fukuoka in a little over two minutes.
Roughly 0.25 times faster than the revolution of the Earth.	
	600 times faster than a housefly.
Roughly 585 times faster than a squid.	300 times faster than a reindeer.
Roughly 1,600 times faster than an octopus.	He would reach Las Vegas in roughly 22 minutes.
Mach 20 is basically faster than most things.	
He moves at Mach 20 and gets drunk at the same speed.	Roughly 108 times faster than Wawrinka's top serve.

Mach 20 is exactly...

Below is a list of comparisons to Koro Sensei's speed which I presented for the character introduction in *Weekly Jump* magazine. Mr. Murakoshi, my editor, came up with these. He was a rookie editor at the beginning, but by the latter half of *Assassination Classroom*, he grasped the essence of the title and was very dependable, coming up with great ideas as well as skillfully supervising tie-in products.

200 times faster than the maximum speed of the Shonan Shinjuku Line train that started halting at Urawa Station this March.	20 times faster than the speed of sound.
135,593 times faster than the TORQ ROADSTER, the fastest three-wheel electric car in the world.	651.341 times faster than Usain Bolt performing the 100-meter dash.
75 times faster than sneezing.	Roughly 146.34 times faster than Randall Johnson's prime-time pitch. Koro Sensei earned the nickname Koro Fire for throwing high and tight pitches at right-handed batters.
3,429 times faster than a lesser emperor dragonfly.	
72,727.27 times faster than the Galápagos tortoise.	Koro Sensei was nicknamed Korostiano Ronaldo after his Mach 20 dashes up the soccer field.
12,000 times faster than the speed of a black mamba attacking you.	
615.38 times faster than the dive of a Peregrine falcon.	88,888.88 times faster than the average rotating sushi. His favorite sushi is Botan shrimp.
Mach 20, but I can't move right now. (Absolute Defense Form in progress).	
Mach 20; however, I can't move right now. (Absolute Defense Form in progress).	400 times faster than a rabbit.
Mach 20, but all I can do is roll when the wind blows. (Absolute Defense Form in progress).	960 times faster than the Sagano Scenic Line.
	151.898 times faster than Irabu's fastest pitch.
Mach 20, but currently I'm on the front line of immobility. (Absolute Defense Form in progress).	He can travel from Tsurumi relay station to Totsuka relay station in roughly 3.48 seconds.
Mach 20, but currently I'm a piece of talking hand luggage. (Absolute Defense Form in progress).	15.18 times faster than the initial muzzle velocity of a bullet fired from a Smith & Wesson M29.44 magnum.
It's hard to believe that I could ever move at Mach 20. (Absolute Defense Form in progress).	153.85 times faster than the fastest pitch of Kazuhisa Ishii, the left-handed specialist.
Apparently, I used to move at Mach 20. (Absolute Defense Form in progress).	Roughly 30,000 times faster than the front of blooming cherry blossom trees moving north.
The talking beach ball. (Absolute Defense Form in progress).	Roughly 133,333.33 times faster than the speed of a cherry blossom petal falling.
Mach 20 after 15 weeks.	
He travels from North Sanriku to Shibuya in roughly 80 seconds.	75 times faster than the "Bucking Bronco/Charging Horse of Tohoku," the Super Komachi, that began its route this March.
He can travel between Haneda and Naha in roughly 230 seconds.	Roughly 58.23 times faster than the SSC Ultimate Aero, which made a comeback as a Guinness World Record this April as the fastest mass-produced car in the world.
170 times faster than the top speed of a bobsled, known as "Formula 1 on Ice."	
480 times faster than an ostrich.	

I haven't lived that long, so I don't have a lot of life experience. But as I worked on this series, I came to believe that everyone has something to teach when they stand up to the podium and take on the role of teacher.

I have been able to bring this series to its conclusion thanks to your support, but I must admit...it is hard for me to part with Koro Sensei. He is a flexible, author-friendly character who adds a touch of humor to any situation.

This octopus-like super creature and his students might change shape and appear before you again someday... For now, though, I will be taking a break, and I hope you will keep me and these characters alive in your hearts.

Thank you for reading this series to the very end.

July 4, 2016
Yusei Matsui

Afterword ①
—The main theme of *Assassination Classroom* is killing your teacher.—

When I created the first couple pages of the first chapter, I immediately realized that the outcome of the story would be tragic.

I thought if I managed to tell the story in a straightforward, well-balanced way without shying away from its core drama, it could become a piece of work that would live on in the hearts of its readers.

Many of the words Koro Sensei bestowed upon his students were not off the top of my head, but based on personal experiences from my short life.

The idea that weak people should use assassination tactics is the same strategy that an unrefined, weak manga artist needs to use to survive in a business filled with great talents. I believe my personal experiences—along with advising my friends about their problems when they've asked me to—have helped me make the problems and solutions in this manga realistic.

ASSASSINATION
CLASSROOM

SHFF

I HOPE YOU CAN KILL ME...

...BEFORE GRADUATION.

RSTL

PWHLEZE

KILL?

?

HM...

?

KILL...

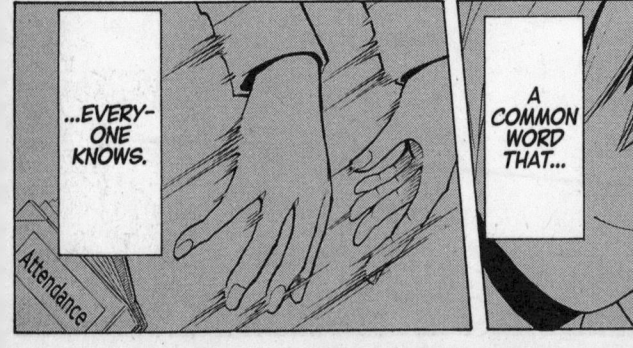

...EVERY-ONE KNOWS.

Attendance

A COMMON WORD THAT...

RING RING RING RING

IF YOU DON'T WANNA GET HURT, YOU BETTER TREAT THIS LIKE A STUDY HALL.

DO YOU KNOW WHAT KIND OF HIGH SCHOOL THIS IS?

KLTTR

HAR HAR HAR HAR HAR!

PWWEASE SIT DOWN...

TH-THE...

...SCHOOL BELL JUST RANG, SO PLEASE SIT DOWN.

SH FF

DON'T ORDER US AROUND.

I'LL KILL YA.

...I'D HARDLY GROW ANY MORE AFTER JUNIOR HIGH.

I NEVER DREAMED...

160 cm

5' 3"

KARMA IS SIX FOOT ONE! HOW IS THAT FAIR?!

Heh heh heh

6' 1"

Tee hee hee

5' 2"

EVERYONE ELSE GOT TALLER.

THE POWER BALANCE IS COMPLETELY THE OPPOSITE OF THE ASSASSINATION CLASSROOM!

ON TOP OF THAT, MY STUDENT TEACHING TERM IS IN THIS AWFUL PLACE...

DIE

DIE DUMBASS KIL

FF

KLTTR

SH

I'LL BE YOUR STUDENT TEACHER THIS SESSION.

NICE TO MEET YOU, EVERYONE!

MY NAME IS NAGISA SHIOTA.

...AND BECOME A TEACHER BELOVED BY ALL MY PUPILS.

I'VE GROWN A LOT TALLER...

SEVEN YEARS HAVE PASSED...

THAT'S WHAT I DREAMED OF, AT LEAST...

NAGISA...

...DOESN'T TAKE ANY NOTICE OF ME.

SO... KAYANO.

HAVE YOU KEPT IN CONTACT WITH HIM?

HOW'S IT GOING WITH NAGISA?

UM...

HE ALWAYS ONLY HAS HIS EYES ON HIS TARGET...

Gokuraku Private High School

HE'S AN ASSASSIN...

...FORGED BY THE COLORFUL BATTLES FOR OUR LIVES...

...!!

A PROUD LIFE.

Budget
¥50,000

A LIFE THAT I HOPE TO RAISE ONE DAY.

A LIFE SHARED WITH OTHERS.

A LIFE DEVOTED TO OTHERS.

DURING THAT YEAR, OUR TEACHER...
...TAUGHT US HOW TO LIVE.
AND THOSE LESSONS ...
...ARE STILL ALIVE WITHIN US.

...WHATEVER PATH WE TAKE...

SP LASH

AND I BET...

...KORO SENSEI WOULD SAY WITH A BIG GRIN ON HIS FACE...

..."IT SUITS YOU PERFECTLY!"

YOU KNOW...

...HAVE ALL HONED THE SKILLS THEY NEED...

THE OTH-ERS...

...TO ACCOM-PLISH THEIR GOALS FOR THE FUTURE.

FWSS

SS

SHHH

...I HEARD THE TOUGH PART COMES AFTER YOU PASS THE EXAM.

BUT...

BY THE WAY, I HEARD KARMA BREEZED THROUGH THE TYPE I CIVIL SERVICE EXAM.

BEING A CIVIL SERVANT CAN BE REALLY STRESSFUL.

THERE'S NOTHING HE CAN'T DO, HUH?

Ministry of Economy, Trade and Industry

RH Slimy Transfusion Blood

THIS COULD...

...SAVE MILLIONS OF PEOPLE, YOU KNOW!

SHE DEVELOPED THIS MOSTLY BY HERSELF.

I'D LIKE TO RUN CLINICAL TRIALS WITH IT.

...CREATING A FORM OF UNIVERSALLY COMPATIBLE ARTIFICIAL BLOOD THAT CAN BE TRANSFUSED INTO PEOPLE OF ANY BLOOD TYPE.

THE TWO OF THEM USED THAT AS THE BASIS FOR...

IN MANAMI AND TAKEBAYASHI'S ADVICE BOOKS...

...KORO SENSEI LEFT THE FORMULA FOR HIS ACTIVE SLIME.

C-come on! We have to watch over them.

okay.

FINAL CLASS TIME TO KILL

Diploma

Dear You,

I hereby award you this
certificate for completing
all the courses of the
Assassination Classroom.

Class 3-E Homeroom Teacher,
Koro Sensei

It's probably like this with them.

PERSON-ALLY, I HOPE...

...THERE'S ONE PERSON IN PARTICULAR...

...WHO WILL USE THIS SCHOOL BUILDING SOMEDAY...

OKANO HAS BEEN USING THE MOUNTAIN.

...BEFORE EVERYONE GETS BUSY JOB HUNTING.

PRESERVING THIS BUILDING IS FINE, BUT WE NEED TO THINK OF A WAY TO PUT THIS PLACE TO GOOD USE...

...AND SHE SAYS THERE'S NO BETTER TRAINING AREA THAN THIS MOUNTAIN.

SHE STARTED HER OWN ACROBATIC PERFORMANCE TEAM AT HER EXERCISE SCIENCE COLLEGE...

SHE'S ALWAYS BEEN GOOD AT EARNING EXTRA CASH, HASN'T SHE?

...HAS BEEN TAKING CHILDREN ON NATURE TOURS HERE FOR A FEE.

KURAHASHI...

THIS ENTIRE PLACE IS A MEMORIAL TO KORO SENSEI.

Nah. It's endless.

Have you finished reading your advice book?

EVERYONE AGREED WE DIDN'T NEED TO MAKE A GRAVE SITE...

Building Depreciation Checklist

...IT DOESN'T FEEL LIKE THEY'RE GONE.

...BECAUSE...

THIS SCHOOL BUILDING...

...MUST BE WHERE THEY RESIDE.

AND THIS IS WHERE EVERYONE RETURNS.

RELAX...

THE SCHOOL RULE IS TO CLEAN THE BUILDING IF IT GETS DIRTY, REMEMBER?

WE BOUGHT THIS MOUNTAIN. IT'S OURS.

SOMEONE'S BEEN TRESPASSING AGAIN.

OKAJIMA! QUIT TAKING SNEAKY SHOTS OF ME AND START CLEANING!

I'M LIVING OFF MY JUNIOR HIGH SCHOOL INHERITANCE.

OH, NOT REALLY...

WHY WOULDN'T SHE BE POPULAR?

SHE'S GOT LOOKS, ACTING CHOPS, CAN DO HER OWN ACTION STUNTS— EVEN JUMP OFF 100-FOOT-HIGH CLIFFS WITH A SMILE ON HER FACE!

NO SURPRISE THERE.

YOU'VE GOTTEN SO FAMOUS, KAYANO!

HEY, MS. TELEVISION STAR!

EVERY-ONE'S HERE...!

I FELT BAD ABOUT LEAVING YOU GUYS TO TAKE CARE OF THIS ALL ON YOUR OWN.

I SNUCK OUT DURING A BREAK.

YOU MUST BE BUSY. IS IT OKAY FOR YOU TO BE HERE?

ARE YOU WEARING YOUR COSTUME?

UH-HUH.

LET'S GET ON WITH THE POLISHING!

ALL RIGHT THEN.

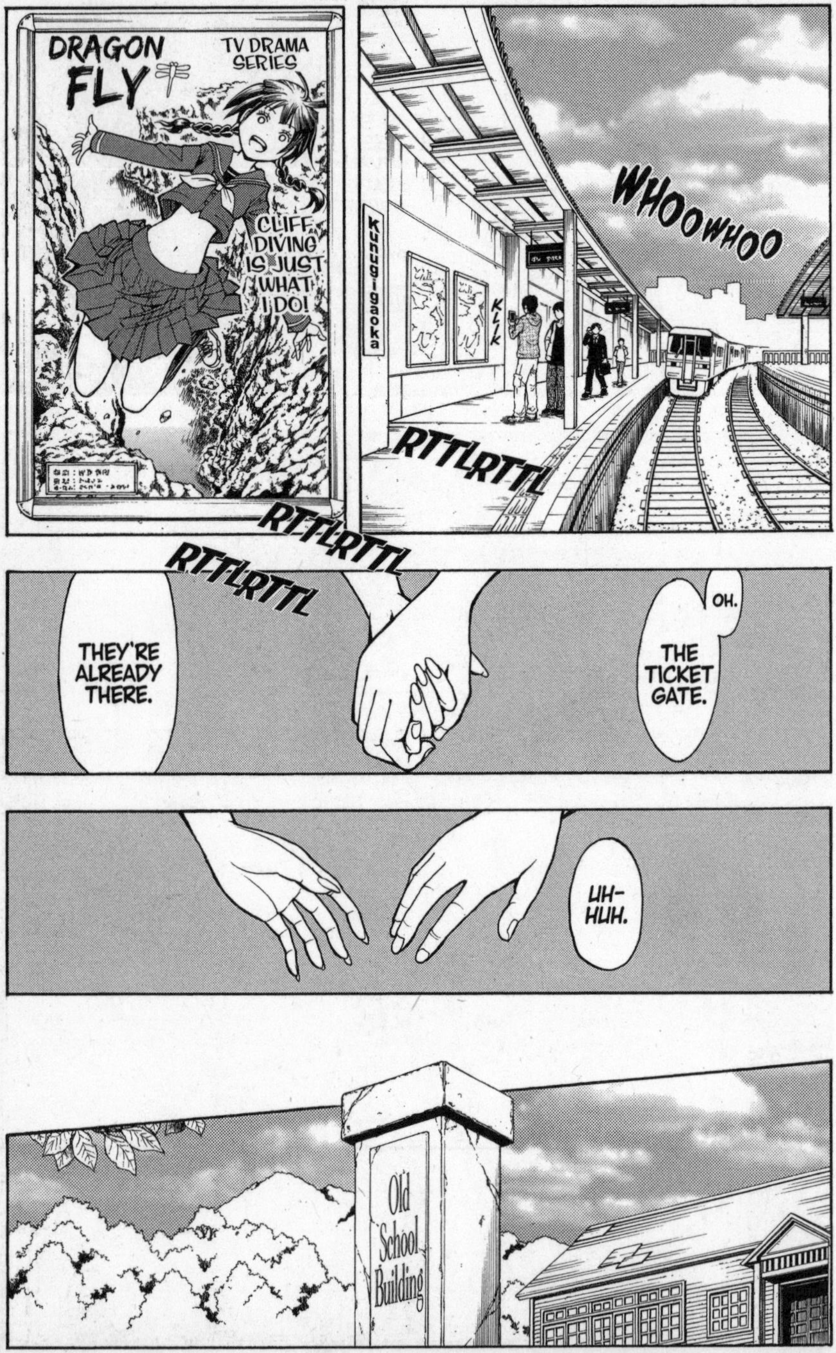

DRAGON FLY

TV DRAMA SERIES

CLIFF DIVING IS JUST WHAT I DO!

WHOOWHOO

RTTLRTTL

RTTLRTTL

RTTLRTTL

THEY'RE ALREADY THERE.

OH. THE TICKET GATE.

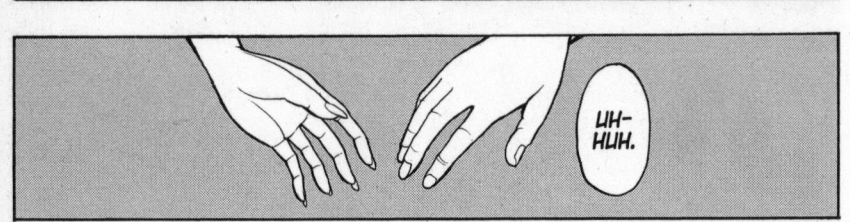

UH-HUH.

Old School Building

...AND SHE HASN'T CHANGED A BIT.

IT'S BEEN SEVEN YEARS SINCE WE MET...

I WONDER HOW THE STUDENTS IRINA AND I TAUGHT...

NO.

...

HOW THE STUDENTS ALL THREE OF US TAUGHT...

Kunugigaoka Station
North Exit

...ARE DOING.

OH WELL...

I GUESS I'LL HAVE TO ASK SOMEONE ELSE TO DO THE JOB.

HUH?! WAI—

BUT IF YOU'RE GOING TO PLAY THAT GAME...

I ASKED YOU TO TAKE ON THIS MISSION BECAUSE I HAVE FAITH IN YOUR PROFESSIONAL ABILITY.

...

...IT'S HARD TO TAKE YOU SERIOUSLY.

COME ON, HONEY!

I JUST WANTED TO MAKE YOU A LITTLE JEALOUS!

I'M KID-DING!!

YESSIR!

THEN MOVE IT!

YES, I'LL GO!

THEN YOU'LL GO?

NOD NOD

AN ORGANIZATION THAT HAS BEEN FOMENTING RIOTS IN THE MIDDLE EAST IS SHOWING SIGNS OF SOME VERY DANGEROUS ACTIVITY.

IRINA...

I NEED YOU TO HEAD OVER THERE TOMORROW.

OKAY.

SURE THING.

EACH NATION HAS DECIDED TO SEND IN AN UNDERCOVER AGENT.

IF A WOMAN AS BEAUTIFUL AS ME WERE TO MEET A HANDSOME RADICAL EXTREMIST OVER THERE...

BUT... I'M WORRIED, DIRECTOR KARASUMA...

TO IMAGINE THE THINGS HE MIGHT DO WITH YOUR WIFE?

MAYBE THAT EXCITES YOU?

OOOH...

THE UNCHANGING CRESCENT MOON SYMBOLIZED OUR YEAR HERE.

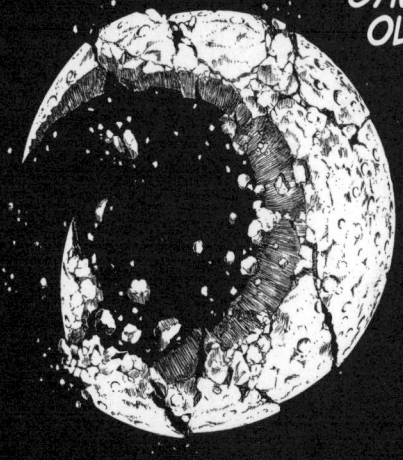

THAT SHAPE WILL GRADUALLY BE FORGOTTEN...

...IS SLOWLY COLLAPSING INTO ITSELF.

THE MOON...

AND SINCE IT WAS DRAWN CLOSER TO EARTH AFTER THE EXPLOSION...

APPARENTLY...

...IT'S DESTINED TO TURN INTO A SMALLER SPHERE THANKS TO ITS GRAVITATIONAL PULL.

...EVENTUALLY...

...WILL BE QUITE SIMILAR TO THE WAY IT WAS BEFORE IT DISINTEGRATED.

...THE SHAPE, SIZE, GRAVITATIONAL PULL AND CYCLE OF THE MOON—FROM THE PERSPECTIVE OF THE EARTH...

WE MADE A FEW DONATIONS HERE AND THERE.

...ENOUGH FOR OUR ACADEMIC FEES AND A SMALL SUM OF MONEY TO GIVE US A HEAD START WHEN THE TIME CAME TO GO OUT ON OUR OWN INTO THE WORLD.

...WE EACH TOOK...

...VERY LARGE PURCHASE...

WE MADE ONE...

WHICH WAS BOUND TO HELP...

...BOLSTER MR. KARASUMA'S REPUTATION.

...WE RETURNED TO THE GOVERNMENT "IN GRATITUDE FOR THEIR SUPPORT THROUGHOUT THE YEAR."

AND THE REST...

MR. KARA-SUMA SAID...

...THE GOVERNMENT WOULD PROBABLY WANT US TO KEEP QUIET ABOUT IT.

THE 300 MILLION DOLLAR BOUNTY WAS SWIFTLY PAID OUT TO CLASS E.

AND WE FOLLOWED KORO SENSEI'S ADVICE FROM THE BOOKS HE LEFT US.

← Incomprehension

WE TALKED IT OVER.

AND SO...

YOU WON'T GROW UP TO BE MATURE ADULTS IF YOU RELY ON MONEY ALONE.

WHAT MATTERS IS WHAT YOU'VE ACCOMPLISHED.

AND IF WE'RE GOING TO DRINK TOGETHER...

...TELL ME WHAT YOU'VE BEEN UP TO AND I'LL TELL YOU ALL ABOUT MY RECENT TROUBLES.

JOIN ME IN A TOAST...

...TO YOUR UNDERCLASSMEN AND ME, AS WE EMBARK ON A NEW JOURNEY!

THDK

...WHATEVER YOU HAVE TO SAY!

WE'LL GLADLY LISTEN TO...

WE HEARD ABOUT ALL THE TROUBLE YOU'VE HAD, MR. ASANO...

...AND ABOUT THE STUDENTS WHO CAME AFTER US.

OH...!

NAGAI.

MORI.

HOW MANY YEARS HAS IT BEEN ...?

IS THERE ANYTHING WE CAN DO TO HELP?

WE'D DO ANYTHING TO REPAY YOU FOR ALL YOU'VE DONE FOR US!

THERE IS **SOME-THING** YOU COULD HELP ME WITH...

WELL THEN ...

RSTL

AFTER WHICH HEAD-MASTER ASANO...

...HAD NO CHOICE BUT TO GIVE UP MANAGEMENT OF THE SCHOOL.

RSTL

KUNUGIGAOKA WAS ACCUSED OF JEOPARDIZING THE LIVES OF ITS STUDENTS...

THE CLASS E SYSTEM WAS JUDGED UNETHICAL AND ABOLISHED.

TH DD

HE'S A MAN OF UNWAVERING RESOLVE AND EXCEPTIONAL TALENT.

...I GET THE FEEL-ING...

BUT...

History of Kunugigaoka 2010

History of

I'M SURE HE'LL BEGIN WORKING IN EDUCATION AGAIN SOMEWHERE VERY SOON...

...THAT WAS ALL PART OF HIS GRAND PLAN.

...MR. ASANO?

CAN WE HELP YOU...

...THE BRILLIANT BRAIN THAT REMAINS INSIDE OF ME.

...THEY COULD STILL MAKE USE OF...

IF PEOPLE WOULD ONLY REALIZE THAT...

Look... it's a beautiful day out.

EVERYONE NEEDS HELP FROM OTHERS TO LIVE.

SHFF

...WAS CLOSED DOWN. WE WERE ITS LAST STUDENTS.

No Trespassing

THE CLASS E SCHOOL BUILDING...

Principal's Office

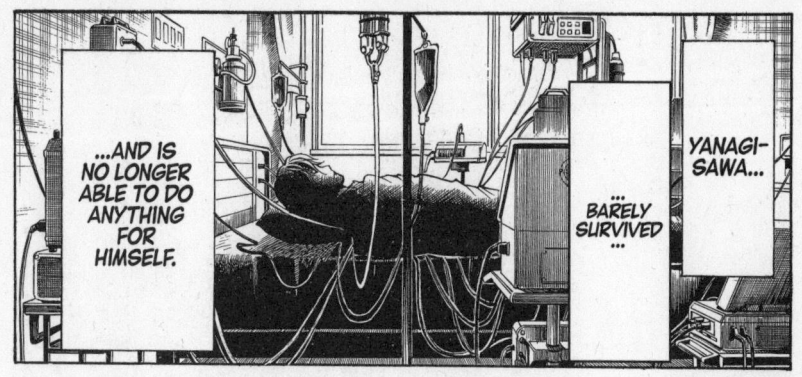

...AND IS NO LONGER ABLE TO DO ANYTHING FOR HIMSELF.

...BARELY SURVIVED...

YANAGI-SAWA...

...AND WAS CONSIDERED UNUSABLE.

...WAS DEEMED TOO UNCONTROLLABLE FOR EITHER CIVILIAN OR MILITARY APPLICATION...

THE RESEARCH HE HAD BEEN CONDUCTING...

MR. YANAGISAWA... I'M HERE TO CHANGE OUT SOME THINGS.

KLTTR KLTTR

...

AFTER THAT...

during the game
was Sugino!
e put some snap onto the b

▲ Dried Bonito with Soy Sauce

Soy Simmered Nori

Japanese butterbur scapes with Miso ▲

One of my favorite photos! The training on this day was extra strenuous, so my handmade rice balls were quite welcome I'm sure. By the way, I placed your favorite filling in each of your personalized rice balls. Check the next page for the recipes for all twenty-eight fillings! ▶

...SO MANY THINGS HAPPENED.

CLASS 179   TIME PASSES

In the end, printed paper wasn't enough.

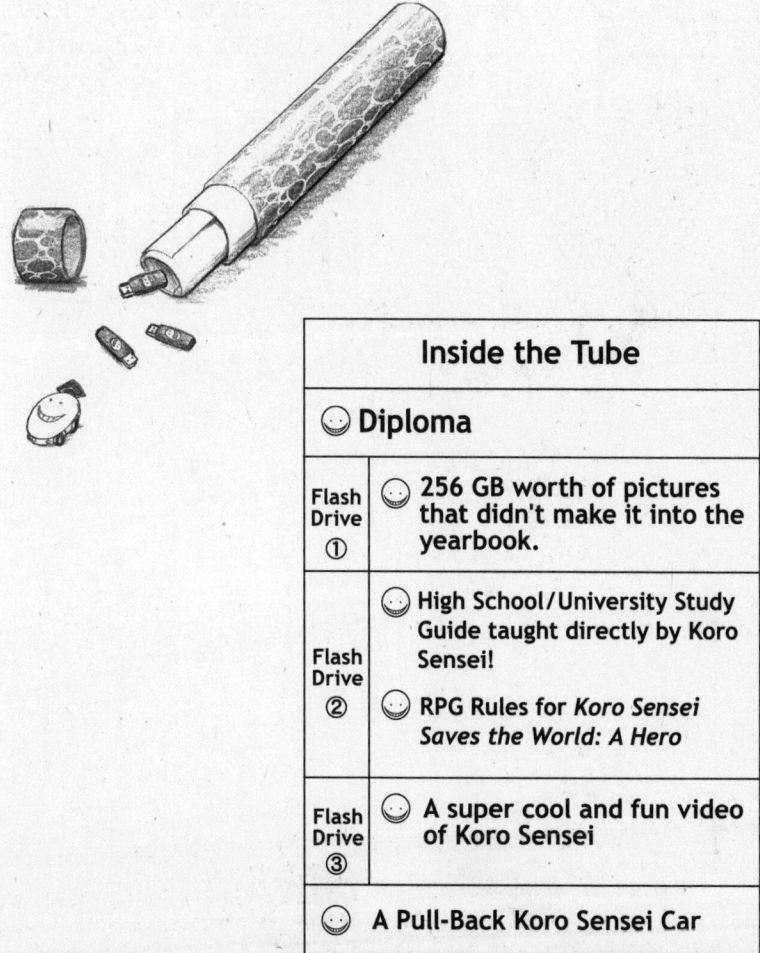

Inside the Tube	
😊 **Diploma**	
Flash Drive ①	😊 **256 GB worth of pictures that didn't make it into the yearbook.**
Flash Drive ②	😊 **High School/University Study Guide taught directly by Koro Sensei!** 😊 **RPG Rules for *Koro Sensei Saves the World: A Hero***
Flash Drive ③	😊 **A super cool and fun video of Koro Sensei**
😊 **A Pull-Back Koro Sensei Car**	

...KORO SENSEI.

GOOD-BYE...

GOOD-BYE...

...KUNUGI-GAOKA JUNIOR HIGH!!

FINE BY ME.

BUT I THINK YOU'RE TOO HARDHEADED TO UNDERSTAND IT ALL, ASANO.

SEE YA!

C'MON, GET ON!

...THIS SO-CALLED KORO SENSEI...

...ABOUT THE HOMEROOM TEACHER WHO BROUGHT YOU TO THIS LEVEL...

...WHEN I CRY OVER SO MANY THINGS.

Hmm.

...

I'LL PROBABLY NEVER HAVE A DAY LIKE THIS AGAIN...

MOST OF YOU WILL BE PERFECT STRANGERS TO ME AFTER THIS.

KRNCH
KRNCH

LET US ESCORT YOU TO THE PARKING LOT.

HIDE BEHIND US.

HERE...

GRAB

BUT FOR TODAY, WE'RE *CLASSMATES*. WE STUDIED AT THE SAME SCHOOL, AFTER ALL.

AND IT WOULD BE A SHAME FOR OUR SCHOOL'S LEADER TO ABANDON YOU NOW.

ONCE THINGS HAVE CALMED DOWN...

...YOU HAD BETTER ANSWER MY QUESTIONS...

I HEAR YOU'RE THE ONLY ONE STAYING BEHIND AT KUNUGI-GAOKA.

AKA-BANE...

MARCH **MARCH** **MARCH**

Kunugigaoka School

MAYBE I'LL EDIT THIS FOOTAGE, UPLOAD IT AND WATCH IT GO VIRAL.

YOU'VE CAUSED A LOT OF TROUBLE FOR US WITH YOUR INTERVIEWS, YOU KNOW.

I'VE MEMORIZED ALL OF YOUR FACES TOO. HYUK HYUK HYUK!

PSH

WHO ARE YOU PEOPLE?! STOP CUTTING US OFF!

WHAT THE ...?

YOU'RE THE ONES BUTTING INTO OUR GRADUA-TION.

CAN'T YOU TELL? WE'RE GRADU-ATES. WE BELONG HERE.

WHAT ARE YOU FEELING IN THIS MOMENT?!

TALK TO US!

DID YOU REALLY KILL THAT MONSTER?!

FASH

FASH

I HAVE A BUS WAITING THERE FOR YOU.

TO THE PARKING LOT! HURRY!

HEY, YOU'RE GETTING IN OUR WAY!

RAHRR

RAHRR

RAHRR

...!

NO PUSH-ING!

HEY...

B MP

KRNCH

BM

P

WHOA!

HOW BIG IS THE LEGACY...

We'll talk more later.

Go see your friends.

...OUR TEACHER LEFT BEHIND FOR US...?

CLASS E STUDENTS!

MAY WE SPEAK WITH YOU?!

ACK!

SLAM

THE CEREMONY IS OVER!

C'MON, TIME FOR THE INTER- VIEW!

THMP THMP

I'M CONFI-DENT...

YOUR SON IS A FINE YOUNG MAN.

...THAT HE WILL ACHIEVE HIS GOAL NEXT MONTH.

I WOULD LIKE FOR HIS ENTIRE FAMILY...

...TO CONGRATULATE HIM.

...AND START OVER AGAIN.

...WE'VE DECIDED TO TRY OUR HARDEST TOO—LIKE YOU DID...

WE'VE BEEN TALK-ING AND...

...HOW HARD-WORKING AND RESPONSIBLE YOU'VE BECOME.

YOUR TEACHER AND YOUR MOTHER TOLD ME ALL ABOUT...

...AND TAKE CARE. DON'T OVERDO THINGS...

THANK YOU, PRINCIPAL ASANO...

YOU OWE THAT TO YOUR TEACHER.

CONGRATU-LATIONS ON YOUR GRADUA-TION.

YOU HAVE A DETER-MINED LOOK IN YOUR EYES NOW...

CHTTR CHTTR

RAHRAH RAHRAH

HUH ...?

....!

MURMUR

I'LL HAVE TO ASK MY PARENTS TO BRING ME MY UNIFORM.

THE SCHOOL'S BEEN CLOSED DOWN, SO THEY'RE DOING IT AT THE CONVENTION CENTER.

MURMUR

SO WHERE'S THE GRADUATION CEREMONY GOING TO BE HELD?

THEY'VE BEEN TRANSFORMED OVER THIS YEAR.

...BUT THEY'RE TOUGH.

I KNOW THEY'RE HURTING...

Kunugigaoka Junior High Graduation Ceremony

ALL RISE!

KL**O**TT**r**

I'LL MAKE THE ARRANGE- MENTS.

OF COURSE...

THAT'S WHY I'M HERE.

MR. KARASUMA, MS. VITCH...

THANK YOU SO MUCH...

...FOR EVERYTHING YOU'VE TAUGHT US!

...BUT I WOULD LIKE TO APOLOGIZE TO YOU IN ADVANCE.

OF COURSE, I WILL DO EVERYTHING IN MY POWER TO PROTECT YOU TO THE BEST OF MY ABILITY...

WE DON'T WANT TO CAUSE YOU ANY TROUBLE, MR. KARA-SUMA.

WE'LL DO OUR PART TO HELP THINGS SETTLE DOWN QUICKLY.

MR. KARA-SUMA...

WE'LL BE FINE.

OUR DAYS BATTLING EVERYONE FROM THE MAIN SCHOOL BUILDING...

WE WANT TO ATTEND OUR GRADUATION CEREMONY TODAY.

BUT IN RETURN... THERE IS SOMETHING WE WOULD LIKE TO DO.

...ARE ALSO AN IMPORTANT PART OF OUR MEMORIES OF KORO SENSEI.

ADD A SHORT STORY TO IT, AND YOU'LL CREATE AN ENGLISH VOCABULARY BOOK THAT STUDENTS CAN REALLY SINK THEIR TEETH INTO.

...IS SO GOOD I THINK IT OUGHT TO BE PUBLISHED!

THE PROBLEM SET I'VE ADDED IN THE APPENDIX...

HOW ABOUT IF I'M THE DARK VERLORD, AND...

HOW ABOUT IF WE SAY I'M STILL ALIVE AND CREATE A SPIN-OFF MANGA?

TO TELL THE TRUTH, THE ADVICE IS SO DETAILED THAT WE GET TIRED TRYING TO READ IT ALL.

...WE FORGET TO CRY AND FALL ASLEEP.

AND WITHOUT REALIZING IT...

...WE RETURN TO THE CLASSROOM TO LOOK FOR MEMENTOS OF KORO SENSEI...

AFTER THAT...

...AND FIND EVERYONE'S GRADUATION DIPLOMA AND YEARBOOK.

NOT TO MENTION...

...A PERSONAL BOOK OF ADVICE TAILORED TO EACH STUDENT ON OUR DESKS.

Koro Sensei's Advice Book Yukiko Kanzaki Edition ☆

ASSASSINATION MEMORIES

What must I do?

The first thing you must do is to know yourself!

This will be an eye-opening experience! You'll be like an alert meerkat!

And so...

...let's go over your strong points on the next page, Kurahashi!

Yeah!

THE ADVICE BOOK BEGINS AS A MANGA TO MAKE IT EASIER TO READ.

FLP

Koro Sensei's Advice Book Kirara Hazama Edition

CLASS 178 — TIME FOR TEARS

TWEET

TWEET

•••

JUST BECAUSE YOUR ASSASSINATION WAS SUCCESSFUL DOESN'T MEAN YOU'VE WEATHERED THE STORM!

PLORK PLORK PLORK PLORK

LISTEN UP, EVERYONE!

Koro Sensei's Advice

CLASS 178 | TIME FOR TEARS

...I HAVE PREPARED A FEW TIDBITS OF ADVICE TO HELP YOU WITH YOUR FUTURE ENDEAVORS!

IN ORDER TO AVOID GETTING SOFT AND LOSING YOUR EDGE...

Stem Vegetables

These foods are rich in dietary fiber and support your gastrointestinal functions.

How to prepare a bamboo shoot

Read page 2,350 for other uses of rice bran!

Bamboo Shoot

Mountain Asparagus

Lotus Root

FIRST... FOOD!

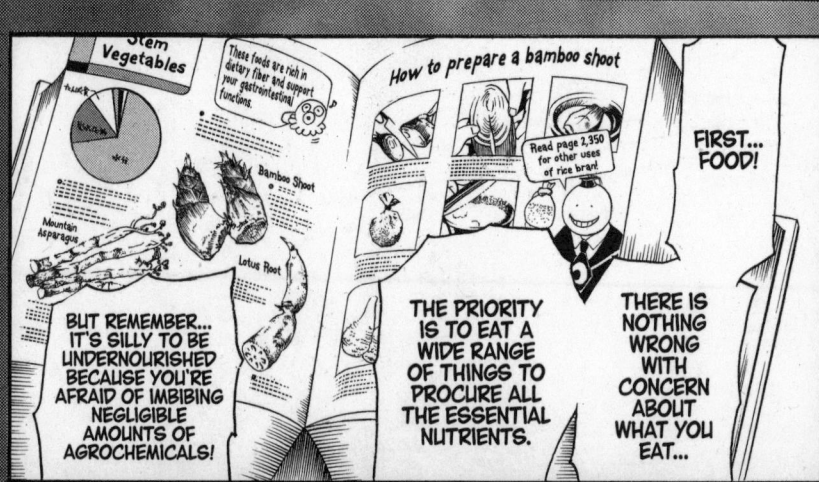

BUT REMEMBER... IT'S SILLY TO BE UNDERNOURISHED BECAUSE YOU'RE AFRAID OF IMBIBING NEGLIGIBLE AMOUNTS OF AGROCHEMICALS!

THE PRIORITY IS TO EAT A WIDE RANGE OF THINGS TO PROCURE ALL THE ESSENTIAL NUTRIENTS.

THERE IS NOTHING WRONG WITH CONCERN ABOUT WHAT YOU EAT...

ASSASSINATION
CLASSROOM 21 CONTENTS

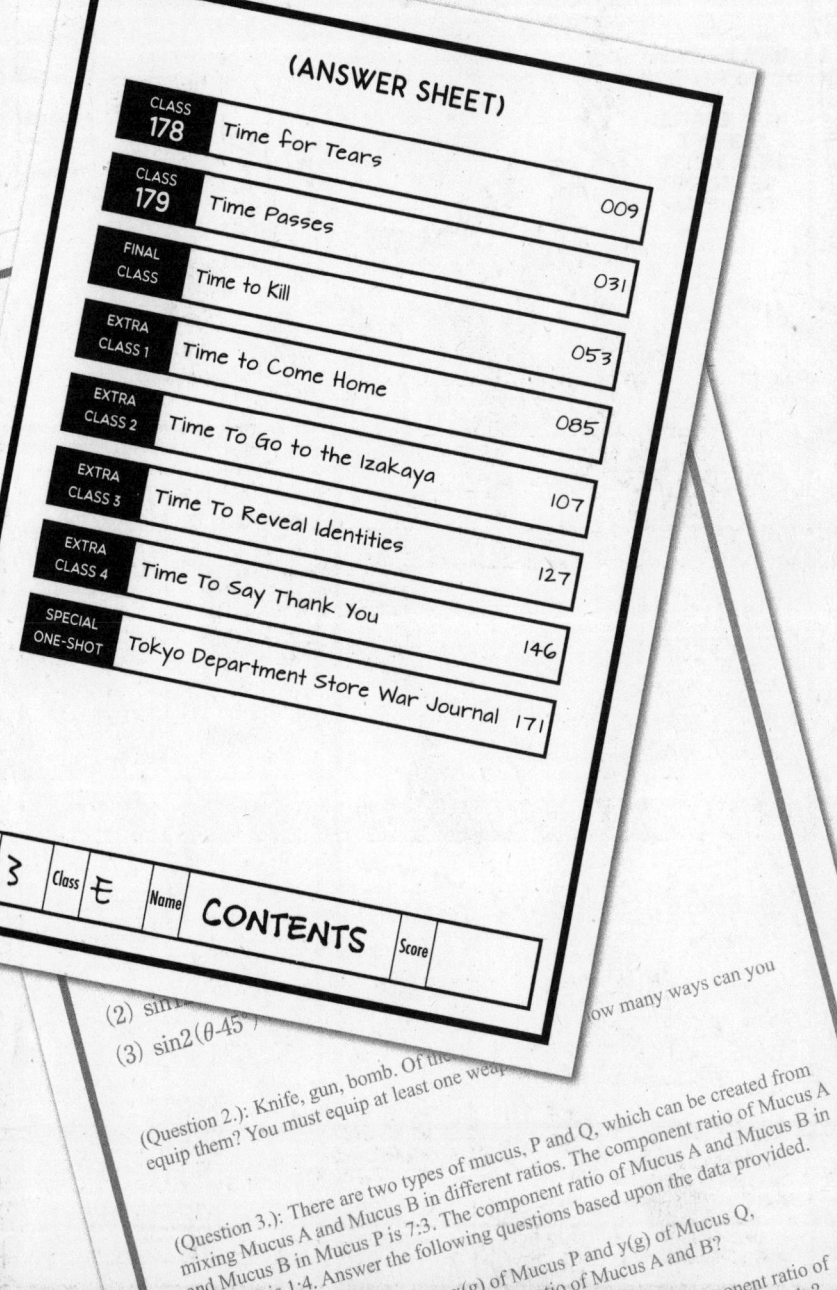

(ANSWER SHEET)

Tokyo Department Store War Journal 171

| Grade 3 | Class E | Name | CONTENTS | Score | |

(2) sin

(3) sin2(θ-45

(Question 2.): Knife, gun, bomb. Of the ... ow many ways can you equip them? You must equip at least one weap...

(Question 3.): There are two types of mucus, P and Q, which can be created from mixing Mucus A and Mucus B in different ratios. The component ratio of Mucus A and Mucus B in Mucus P is 7:3. The component ratio of Mucus A and Mucus B in Mucus Q is 1:4. Answer the following questions based upon the data provided.

...en mixing x(g) of Mucus P and y(g) of Mucus Q,
... component ratio of Mucus A and B?
...has a component ratio of
...ust you do?

Individual Statistics

E-25 Toka Yada

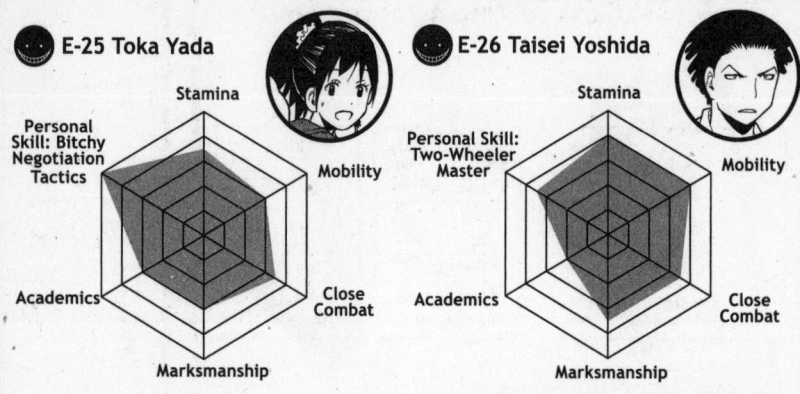

Radar chart axes: Stamina, Mobility, Close Combat, Marksmanship, Academics, Personal Skill: Bitchy Negotiation Tactics

E-26 Taisei Yoshida

Radar chart axes: Stamina, Mobility, Close Combat, Marksmanship, Academics, Personal Skill: Two-Wheeler Master

E-27 Autonomous Intelligence Fixed Artillery

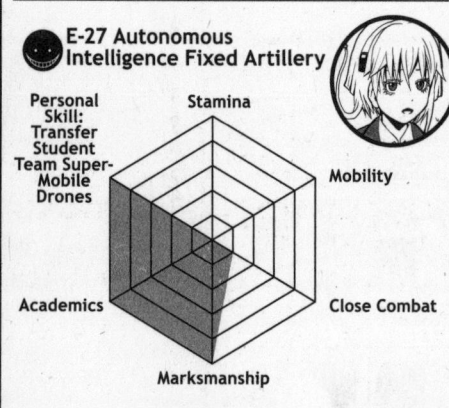

Radar chart axes: Stamina, Mobility, Close Combat, Marksmanship, Academics, Personal Skill: Transfer Student Team Super-Mobile Drones

E-28 Itona Horibe

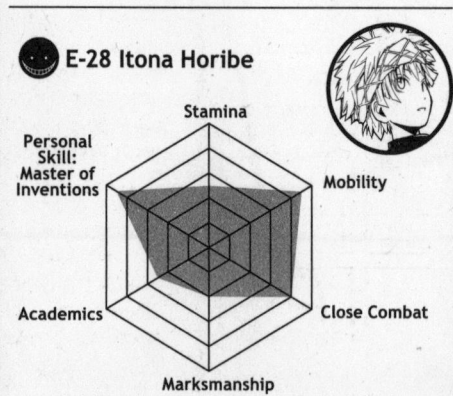

Radar chart axes: Stamina, Mobility, Close Combat, Marksmanship, Academics, Personal Skill: Master of Inventions

E-6 Meg Kataoka	E-22 Hiroto Maehara
E-7 Kaede Kayano	E-11 Nagisa Shiota
E-21 Yuzuki Fuwa	E-13 Tomohito Sugino
E-20 Sumire Hara	E-12 Sosuke Sugaya

E-27 Autonomous Intelligence Fixed Artillery	E-28 Itona Horibe

Kunugigaoka Junior High 3-E
Koro Sensei Class Seating Arrangement

Teacher Koro Sensei

Teacher Tadaomi Karasuma

Teacher Irina Jelavich

Assassination Class Roster

E-4 Hinata Okano

E-2 Yuma Isogai

E-10 Hinano Kurahashi

E-9 Masayoshi Kimura

E-17 Rio Nakamura

E-23 Koki Mimura

E-25 Toka Yada

E-14 Kotaro Takebayashi

E-19 Rinka Hayami

E-3 Taiga Okajima

E-8 Yukiko Kanzaki

E-26 Taisei Yoshida

E-5 Manami Okuda

E-15 Ryunosuke Chiba

E-18 Kirara Hazama

E-24 Takuya Muramatsu

E-1 Karma Akabane

E-16 Ryoma Terasaka

Always assassinate your target using a method that brings a smile to your face.

I am open for assassinations at any time. But don't let them get in the way of your studying.

I won't harm students who try to assassinate me. But if your skills are rusty, expect a good scrubbing.

Nagisa Shiota

pick up!

He was the main character, so obviously he got the spotlight in many scenes; however, everyone in Class 3-E received the same attention from Koro Sensei. Koro Sensei never played favorites.

Karma Akabane

Class E student. He learned to take his studies a bit more seriously after some initial failures and earned first place in the overall school scores on the second semester midterm.

Tadaomi Karasuma

Member of the Ministry of Defense and the Class E students' P.E. teacher. Though serious about his duties, he has successfully built good relationships with his students.

Gakushu Asano

In the end, he learned the truth about Koro Sensei on TV and accepted it. He feels a certain camaraderie with Class E after all the battles they fought against each other throughout the year.

Koro Tribune Final Issue!

These articles were mainly written by Fuwa and occasionally by Okajima, Hazama, Takebayashi and others. Look for more from them in the future!

Saying goodbye is hard.

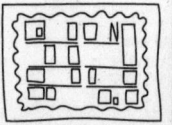

Irina Jelavich

A sexy assassin hired as an English teacher. She's known for using her "womanly charms" to get close to a target. Karasuma has finally admitted that he reciprocates her feelings for him and they have moved in together.

...powerful enough to mutate your body!

Burn fat with bio-shocks...

Yanagisawa's Special Sauna Suit

Gakuho Asano

The principal of Kunugigaoka Academy. Deep down, he and Koro Sensei are two of a kind—that's why he is both a formidable enemy as well as Koro Sensei's greatest supporter.

...THAT I MUST STAKE MY LIFE ON TEACHING THE ASSASSINATION CLASSROOM.

AFTER GIVING IT A GREAT DEAL OF THOUGHT, THE ANSWER I ARRIVED AT WAS...

Story Thus Far

Kunugigaoka Junior High Class 3-E is taught by a monster who even the armies of the world with all their state-of-the-art technology can't kill. That monster, Koro Sensei, is fated to self-destruct and take planet Earth with him, so...

...a bounty has been placed on his head. It comes down to his students in 3-E, the so-called "End Class." Once looked down upon by the rest of the school, this class of misfits is now respected for the athleticism and powers of concentration they have developed thanks to the dedicated instruction of Koro Sensei and Mr. Karasuma of the Ministry of Defense. A strong bond has formed between the students and Koro Sensei, transcending their relationship as assassins and targets. But the time to say farewell has finally arrived... Faced with the inevitability of the world's militaries' specially designed laser delivering the coup de grace to their beloved teacher, Class E assassinates Koro Sensei themselves. What have they learned over this year? What will live on in their hearts? And how will they move on into the future..?

Thank you for everything, Koro Sensei...

Koro Tribune

Final Issue

Published by: Class 3-E Newspaper Staff

Koro Sensei

THEY ARE NEITHER A WEAKNESS NOR A BURDEN!

THEY ARE MY STUDENTS!

He's so cool...

A mysterious, man-made, octopus-like creature whose name is a play on the words "koro senai," which means "can't kill." He is capable of flying at Mach 20 and his versatile tentacles protect him from attacks and aid him in everyday activities. He followed in the footsteps of Aguri, the woman who saved his humanity, by becoming the teacher of Class 3-E.

Kaede Kayano

Class E student. She enrolled in Class E to avenge her sister's death by killing Koro Sensei. She was once a child actress prodigy. Many people in show business hope to see her make a comeback.

Nagisa Shiota

Class E student. He has a hidden talent for assassinations and decides to hone those skills to help others.

His dream is to become a teacher like Koro Sensei someday.

No one objected...

when he took on the role.

ASSASSINATION CLASSROOM

21

TIME TO SAY THANK YOU

YUSEI MATSUI

SHONEN JUMP ADVANCED